INTRODUCING
ISSUES WITH
OPPOSING
VIEWPOINTS®

Vaccines

Noël Merino, *Book Editor*

GREENHAVEN PRESS
A part of Gale, Cengage Learning

GALE
CENGAGE Learning™

Detroit • New York • San Francisco • New Haven, Conn • Waterville, Maine • London

Christine Nasso, *Publisher*
Elizabeth Des Chenes, *Managing Editor*

For more information, contact:
Greenhaven Press
27500 Drake Rd.
Farmington Hills, MI 48331-3535
Or you can visit our Internet site at gale.cengage.com

For product information and technology assistance, contact us at

Gale Customer Support, 1-800-877-4253
For permission to use material from this text or product, submit all requests online at
www.cengage.com/permissions

Further permissions questions can be e-mailed to permissionrequest@cengage.com

Articles in Greenhaven Press anthologies are often edited for length to meet page requirements. In addition, original titles of these works are changed to clearly present the main thesis and to explicitly indicate the author's opinion. Every effort is made to ensure that Greenhaven Press accurately reflects the original intent of the authors. Every effort has been made to trace the owners of copyrighted material.

LIBRARY OF CONGRESS CATALOGING-IN-PUBLICATION DATA

Vaccines / Noël Merino, book editor.
   p. cm. -- (Introducing issues with opposing viewpoints)
Includes bibliographical references and index.
ISBN 978-0-7377-5204-5 (hardcover)
1. Vaccines--Juvenile literature. 2. Vaccination--Juvenile literature. I. Merino, Noël.
RA638.V332 2011
615'.372--dc22

                                                    2010040832

Printed in the United States of America
1 2 3 4 5 6 7 15 14 13 12 11

Contents

Chapter 3: How Can Vaccines Be Improved?

Foreword

Indulging in a wide spectrum of ideas, beliefs, and perspectives is a critical cornerstone of democracy. After all, it is often debates over differences of opinion, such as whether to legalize abortion, how to treat prisoners, or when to enact the death penalty, that shape our society and drive it forward. Such diversity of thought is frequently regarded as the hallmark of a healthy and civilized culture. As the Reverend Clifford Schutjer of the First Congregational Church in Mansfield, Ohio, declared in a 2001 sermon, "Surrounding oneself with only like-minded people, restricting what we listen to or read only to what we find agreeable is irresponsible. Refusing to entertain doubts once we make up our minds is a subtle but deadly form of arrogance." With this advice in mind, Introducing Issues with Opposing Viewpoints books aim to open readers' minds to the critically divergent views that comprise our world's most important debates.

Introducing Issues with Opposing Viewpoints simplifies for students the enormous and often overwhelming mass of material now available via print and electronic media. Collected in every volume is an array of opinions that captures the essence of a particular controversy or topic. Introducing Issues with Opposing Viewpoints books embody the spirit of nineteenth-century journalist Charles A. Dana's axiom: "Fight for your opinions, but do not believe that they contain the whole truth, or the only truth." Absorbing such contrasting opinions teaches students to analyze the strength of an argument and compare it to its opposition. From this process readers can inform and strengthen their own opinions, or be exposed to new information that will change their minds. Introducing Issues with Opposing Viewpoints is a mosaic of different voices. The authors are statesmen, pundits, academics, journalists, corporations, and ordinary people who have felt compelled to share their experiences and ideas in a public forum. Their words have been collected from newspapers, journals, books, speeches, interviews, and the Internet, the fastest growing body of opinionated material in the world.

Introducing Issues with Opposing Viewpoints shares many of the well-known features of its critically acclaimed parent series, Opposing Viewpoints. The articles are presented in a pro/con format, allowing readers to absorb divergent perspectives side by side. Active reading questions preface each viewpoint, requiring the student to approach the material thoughtfully and carefully. Useful charts, graphs, and cartoons supplement each article. A thorough introduction provides readers with crucial background on an issue. An annotated bibliography points the reader toward articles, books, and websites that contain additional information on the topic. An appendix of organizations to contact contains a wide variety of charities, nonprofit organizations, political groups, and private enterprises that each hold a position on the issue at hand. Finally, a comprehensive index allows readers to locate content quickly and efficiently.

Introducing Issues with Opposing Viewpoints is also significantly different from Opposing Viewpoints. As the series title implies, its presentation will help introduce students to the concept of opposing viewpoints and learn to use this material to aid in critical writing and debate. The series' four-color, accessible format makes the books attractive and inviting to readers of all levels. In addition, each viewpoint has been carefully edited to maximize a reader's understanding of the content. Short but thorough viewpoints capture the essence of an argument. A substantial, thought-provoking essay question placed at the end of each viewpoint asks the student to further investigate the issues raised in the viewpoint, compare and contrast two authors' arguments, or consider how one might go about forming an opinion on the topic at hand. Each viewpoint contains sidebars that include at-a-glance information and handy statistics. A Facts About section located in the back of the book further supplies students with relevant facts and figures.

Following in the tradition of the Opposing Viewpoints series, Greenhaven Press continues to provide readers with invaluable exposure to the controversial issues that shape our world. As John Stuart Mill once wrote: "The only way in which a human being can make some approach to knowing the whole of a subject is by hearing what can be said about it by persons of every variety of opinion and studying all modes in which it can be looked at by every character of mind. No wise man ever acquired his wisdom in any mode but this." It is to this principle that Introducing Issues with Opposing Viewpoints books are dedicated.

Introduction

"There are many reasons for the current antivaccination activity."

—Kurt Link, *The Vaccine Controversy: The History, Use, and Safety of Vaccinations.* Westport, CT: Praeger, 2005.

Vaccines were first developed in the late eighteenth century. Vaccines became popular in the nineteenth century, with the first laws passed regarding vaccination. Numerous vaccines were produced in the twentieth century, including those for polio, measles, mumps, and rubella. Despite the fact that vaccines are widely credited with eradicating smallpox and drastically reducing the incidence of polio, they have always been a source of controversy. Opponents of vaccines charge that they are ineffective or unsafe, or that mandating vaccination violates personal or religious liberty. This controversy continues today, with the most recent controversy centering on the alleged link between vaccines and autism.

According to the American Psychiatric Association's *Diagnostic and Statistical Manual of Mental Disorders,* fourth edition, text revision (*DSM-IV-TR*), an autism spectrum disorder is a psychological condition that is marked by "impairment in social interaction," "qualitative impairments in communication," and "restricted repetitive and stereotyped patterns of behavior, interests, and activities."[1] The number of reported autism spectrum disorders (ASDs) increased dramatically in the 1990s and 2000s. The Centers for Disease Control and Prevention (CDC) reports, "The average total ASD prevalence in 2006 (children born in 1998) was 9.0 per 1,000 children, which translates to one in 110 children."[2] Although the CDC reports that "no single factor explains the changes in identified ASD prevalence," many people believe that there is a link between the rise in autism and childhood vaccination. Part of this belief stems from a British study performed in the late twentieth century.

British researcher Andrew Wakefield published a study in 1998 in the British medical journal the *Lancet,* suggesting a possible link between the measles, mumps, and rubella vaccine (MMR) and ASDs.

When the study was published, Wakefield and his colleagues held a press conference and suggested that parents continue with vaccination of measles, mumps, and rubella, but do so with single vaccinations rather than the three-in-one MMR. The study, Wakefield's suggestion to parents, and the associated media attention is believed to have caused a drop in the number of parents who vaccinated their children from the disease.

In 2004 the British General Medical Council (GMC) announced an inquiry into possible misconduct by Wakefield and his colleagues during their study. In 2010 the GMC found that Wakefield and his colleagues had acted "dishonestly and irresponsibly."[3] In February 2010 *The Lancet* retracted Wakefield's 1998 publication, and in May 2010 he was struck from the United Kingdom's medical register. Wakefield responded by publishing *Callous Disregard: Autism and Vaccines—the Truth Behind a Tragedy,* a book in which he tells the story, in his words, of "a struggle against compromise in medicine, corruption of science, and a real and present threat to children in the interests of policy and profit."[4] Wakefield continues to argue for more research on the possible link between autism and vaccines.

Beyond the specific concerns about the MMR vaccine raised by Wakefield, concerns have been raised about the safety of the mercury-based preservative, thimerosal, used in vaccines. One of the leading proponents of this view is the Coalition for SafeMinds, an organization founded in 2000 working to, in their words, "restore health and protect future generations by eradicating the devastation of autism and associated health disorders induced by mercury and other man made toxicants."[5] In 1999 the CDC and American Academy of Pediatrics made a recommendation to vaccine makers to remove all thimerosal from vaccines, simply as a precautionary measure. As a result, according to the US Food and Drug Administration, "Since 2001, all vaccines recommended for children 6 years of age and younger have contained either no thimerosal or only trace amounts, with the exception of inactivated influenza vaccines, which are marketed in both the preservative-free and thimerosal-preservative-containing formulations."[6] This action, however, had the unintended effect of making parents even more concerned about vaccines.

In the United States, the Immunization Safety Review Committee of the Institute of Medicine—an independent, nonprofit organization—published a study in 2004 that disputed connections between vaccines and autism. The committee concluded: "The evidence favors rejection of a causal relationship between thimerosal-containing vaccines and autism," and "the evidence favors rejection of a causal relationship between MMR vaccine and autism."[7] Despite this report by the Immunization Safety Review Committee, one in four US parents believes some vaccines cause autism in healthy children, according to a University of Michigan study done in 2009.

The controversy about vaccines that has existed since their inception continues today. There is an ongoing debate about the effectiveness of vaccines and whether their benefits outweigh the risks. There is a similar debate about whether vaccinations should be mandatory for children attending public school. In addition, there is a debate about whether pursuing the development of vaccines is the best way to deal with public health crises. These fascinating debates and others are explored in *Introducing Issues with Opposing Viewpoints: Vaccines.*

Notes

1. American Psychiatric Association, "299.00 Autistic Disorder," in *Diagnostic and Statistical Manual of Mental Disorders,* 4th ed., rev. text. Washington, DC: American Psychiatric Association, 2000.
2. Centers for Diseases Control and Prevention, "CDC Study: An Average of 1 in 110 Children Have an ASD," April 12, 2010. www.cdc.gov.
3. Quoted in Nick Triggle, "MMR Scare Doctor 'Acted Unethically,' Panel Finds," BBC News, January 28, 2010. http://news.bbc .co.uk/2/hi/health/8483865.stm..
4. Andrew J. Wakefield, *Callous Disregard: Autism and Vaccine—the Truth Behind a Tragedy.* New York: Skyhorse, 2010.
5. SafeMinds, "Welcome." www.safeminds.org.
6. US Food and Drug Administration, "Thimerosal in Vaccines Questions and Answers," May 1, 2009. www.fda.gov/Biologics BloodVaccines/Vaccines/QuestionsaboutVaccines/ucm070430 .htm.
7. Immunization Safety Review Committee, *Immunization Safety Review: Vaccines Autism.* Washington, DC: National Academies Press, 2004, p. 16.

Chapter 1

Do Vaccines Do More Harm Than Good?

A teenager receives a vaccination to protect against the human papillomavirus. Vaccinations are the subject of much controversy.

Viewpoint

1

The Harms of Vaccines Are Widespread and Underreported

Neil Z. Miller

"The general public is essentially unaware of the true number of people— mostly children— who have been permanently damaged or died after receiving several vaccines at the same time."

In the following viewpoint Neil Z. Miller contends that babies are overdosed with vaccines. Miller claims that the numerous vaccines given to young children are full of harmful ingredients. Furthermore, he argues that babies are given too many vaccines in too short a period of time. Miller argues that vaccines have not been adequately tested for safety and that their administration can cause serious adverse reactions. He also claims that adverse reactions to vaccines are underreported. Miller is the director of the ThinkTwice Global Vaccine Institute and the author of *Vaccine Safety Manual for Concerned Families and Health Practitioners*.

Parents need to understand that vaccines are drugs. They contain antigens, preservatives, adjuvants, stabilizers, antibiotics, buffers, diluents, emulsifiers, and inactivating chemicals. They also contain residue from animal and human growth mediums. Here is a partial list of vaccine ingredients, with brief comments:

Vaccine Ingredients

These are the main components of any vaccine, designed to induce an immune response. They are either weakened germs or fragments of the disease organism: viruses (polio), bacteria (*Bordetella pertussis*), and toxoids (*Clostridium tetani*) are examples.

Growth mediums: Viruses require a medium in which to propagate, or reproduce. Common broths include chick embryo fibroblasts; chick kidney cells; mouse brains; African green monkey kidney cells; and human diploid cells cultured from aborted human fetuses.

Adjuvants: These are used to enhance immunity. Aluminum salts are the most common and have been linked to neurological disorders.

Preservatives: These are used to stop microbial contamination of vaccines. Thimerosal (mercury) is a recognized developmental toxin and suspected immune, kidney, skin and sense organ toxin. Benzethonium chloride is a suspected endocrine, skin and sense organ toxin. 2-phenoxyethanol is a suspected developmental and reproductive toxin. It is also chemically similar to antifreeze. Phenol is a suspected blood, developmental, liver, kidney, neuro, reproductive, respiratory, skin and sense organ toxin.

Stabilizers: These are used to inhibit chemical reactions and prevent vaccine contents from separating or sticking to the vial. Fetal bovine (calf) serum is a commonly used stabilizer. Monosodium glutamate

(MSG) helps the vaccine remain unchanged when exposed to heat, light, acidity, or humidity. Human serum albumin helps stabilize live viruses. Porcine (pig) gelatin, which protects vaccines from freeze-drying or heat, can cause severe allergic reactions.

Antibiotics: These are added to prevent bacterial growth during vaccine production and storage. Neomycin is a developmental toxin and suspected neurotoxin. Streptomycin is a suspected blood, skin and sense organ toxin. Polymyxin B is a suspected liver and kidney toxin.

Additives, Chemicals, and Contaminants in Vaccines

Additives (buffers, diluents, emulsifiers, excipients, residuals, solvents, etc.): Some of these, such as sodium chloride, are probably benign. Others, such as egg proteins and yeast can cause severe reactions. Ammonium sulfate is a suspected liver, neuro and respiratory toxin. Glycerin is a suspected blood, liver and neuro toxin. Sodium borate is a suspected blood, endocrine, liver and neuro toxin. Polysorbate 80 is a suspected skin and sense organ toxin. Hydrochloric acid (added to some vaccines to balance pH) is a suspected liver, immune, loco-motor, respiratory, skin and sense organ toxin. Sodium hydroxide is a suspected respiratory, skin and sense organ toxin. Potassium chloride is a suspected blood, liver and respiratory toxin.

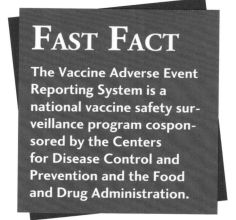

FAST FACT

The Vaccine Adverse Event Reporting System is a national vaccine safety surveillance program cosponsored by the Centers for Disease Control and Prevention and the Food and Drug Administration.

Inactivating chemicals: These kill unwanted viruses and bacteria that could contaminate vaccines. Formaldehyde (or formalin) is a known carcinogen and suspected liver, immune, neuro, reproductive, respiratory, skin and sense organ toxin. It is also used in embalming fluids. Glutaraldehyde is a suspected developmental, immune, reproductive, respiratory, skin and sense organ toxin. Polyoxyethylene is a suspected endocrine toxin.

Contaminants: Vaccines may also contain dangerous, unintended substances, such as the carcinogenic monkey virus, SV-40, found in some polio vaccines, and HIV discovered in early hepatitis B vaccines.

The Number of Vaccines Given to Babies

Today, children receive one vaccine at birth, eight vaccines at two months, eight vaccines at four months, nine vaccines at six months, and twelve additional vaccines between 12 and 18 months. The pure and innocent baby is overdosed with 38 vaccine/drugs by the time he or she is 1½ years old!

According to the Centers for Disease Control and Prevention (CDC), babies should get the following vaccine/drug doses before they reach 18 months of age:

- up to 4 doses of the hepatitis B vaccine
- 3 doses of the rotavirus vaccine
- 4 doses of the DTaP shot (for diphtheria, tetanus and pertussis)
- 4 doses of the Hib vaccine (haemophilus influenzae Type B)
- 4 doses of the pneumococcal vaccine (PCV/Prevnar)
- 3 doses of the polio vaccine
- up to 2 doses of the flu vaccine
- 2 doses of the hepatitis A vaccine
- 1 MMR shot (for measles, mumps and rubella)
- 1 chickenpox vaccine

Babies receive *several* vaccines at each doctor visit. *Many babies receive 8 or more vaccines simultaneously* at 2, 4 and 6 months of age. Imagine ingesting eight or nine drugs all at once. That's what babies are getting. In fact, these babies are not *ingesting* the drugs; instead, the drugs are being *injected* directly into their tiny bloodstreams.

Many babies receive *more* than eight or nine vaccines at once. Since some shot dates are variable (due to "age range" flexibility built into the immunization schedule), *it is permissible for babies to receive a cocktail of up to 13 vaccines/drugs at their 12-month or 15-month doctor visits!*

The vaccines recommended at these ages include DTaP (diphtheria, tetanus, pertussis), hepatitis B, Hib, PCV, polio, flu, MMR (measles, mumps, rubella), chickenpox, and hepatitis A. Up to seven vaccines (for DTaP, hepatitis B, polio, flu, and hepatitis A) can be administered to babies at 18 months.

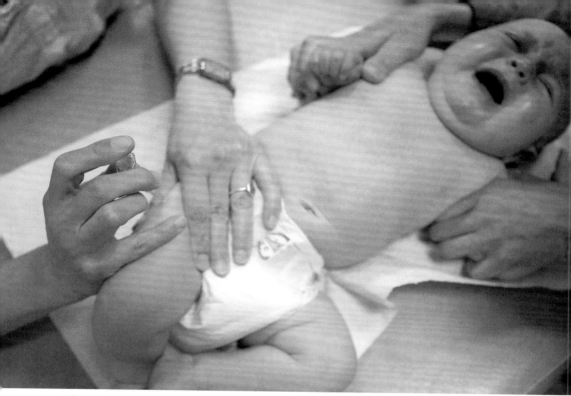

A four-month-old girl receives a round of vaccinations. By the age of eighteen months, most infants have received thirty-eight different vaccinations.

The Safety of Vaccines

Several vaccines are administered simultaneously for *convenience*, not safety. Authorities believe that parents are less likely to fully vaccinate their children if they have to make extra trips to the doctor's office. In fact, vaccine manufacturers are not required to test their products in all of the various combinations that they are likely to be used. In addition, vaccines are not adjusted for the weight of the child. For example, a 6-pound newborn receives the same dose of hepatitis B vaccine—with the same amount of aluminum and formaldehyde—as a 12-pound toddler. It is also important to note that babies are not screened prior to vaccination to determine which ones may be more susceptible to an adverse reaction.

Dr. Russell Blaylock has studied toxic synergy. He notes that when two weakly toxic pesticides are used alone, neither causes Parkinson's syndrome in experimental animals. However, when they are combined, they can cause the full-blown disease quite rapidly. He likens this to multiple vaccines administered simultaneously:

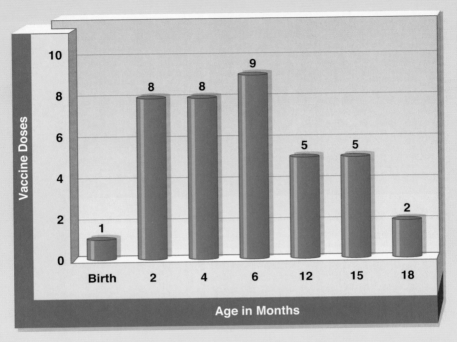

Babies Receive 38 Vaccines by 18 Months of Age

Vaccine Doses / Age in Months

Taken from: Centers for Disease Control and Prevention Immunization Schedule.

"Vaccinations, if too numerous and spaced too close together, act like chronic illness."

For similar reasons, Drs. Andrew Wakefield and Stephanie Cave also suggested spacing some vaccines apart (MMR, for example) to lessen the potentially excessive immunological burden on the body. However, it's important to understand that this strategy will not guarantee protection against serious—or even fatal—side effects. Every "body" is different; no two people react the same way. *Single vaccines given separately can, and often do, cause adverse reactions.*

The Damage Done by Vaccines

The general public is essentially unaware of the true number of people—mostly children—who have been permanently damaged or died after receiving several vaccines at the same time. *Every year more than 20,000 vaccine adverse reaction reports are filed with the federal government.* These include emergency hospitalizations, irreversible injuries, and deaths. Still, these numbers may be grossly underreported because the FDA [US Food and Drug Administration] estimates that 90 percent of doctors do not report reactions. A confidential study conducted by Connaught Laboratories, a vaccine manufacturer, indicated that "a *fifty-fold* underreporting of adverse events" is likely. Yet, even this figure may be conservative. According to Dr. David Kessler, former director of the FDA, "only about one percent of serious events [adverse drug reactions] are reported." (Multiply reported vaccine reactions by 100 for a more accurate sum.)

The FDA and CDC jointly operate a national database where doctors, nurses and concerned parents can report suspected reactions to vaccines. *These reports—340,000 to date—include children who have been permanently damaged or died after receiving several vaccines simultaneously.*

EVALUATING THE AUTHOR'S ARGUMENTS:

In this viewpoint Neil Z. Miller claims that adverse reactions to vaccines may be one hundred times the number reported. Assuming this is true, how might a proponent of the current vaccination recommendations argue that this level of risk is acceptable?

The Harms of Vaccines Are Greatly Outweighed by the Benefits

"As common infectious diseases loosen their hold on human beings, so the harms caused by immunisation loom larger and larger in people's minds, obliterating remembrance of conditions before immunisation."

Theodore Dalrymple

In the following viewpoint Theodore Dalrymple argues that it is too easy to forget the harms caused by diseases before the era of vaccines. He believes that people place too much significance on singular harmful events caused by vaccines, forgetting that the vaccines themselves save many lives. Dalrymple compares modern-day resistance to vaccines to resistance years ago, concluding that the resistance today is just as irrational. He claims that people take for granted the benefits of vaccines in today's world, allowing them to be inappropriately mistrustful of vaccines. Dalrymple is a retired doctor and the author of *An Intelligent Person's Guide to Medicine.*

AS YOU READ, CONSIDER THE FOLLOWING QUESTIONS:
  1. The author claims that it has been estimated that the vaccine against cervical cancer will cause what proportion of deaths?
  2. Dalrymple contends that there was a widespread movement against vaccination in England during what time period?
  3. The author gives what explanation for the phenomenon of people counting one death from a vaccine as more significant than one thousand lives saved by the vaccine?

When I was 6, very shortly before polio vaccine was released, my best friend, from whom I was inseparable, contracted the disease, and was permanently paralysed from the waist down. Unbeknown to me, my parents lived many weeks of terrible anxiety on my behalf. This is an anxiety that no parent now has to experience, thanks to the vaccine.

But as a medical student, I saw a case of generalised vaccinia (the active virus in the smallpox vaccine) and never forgot it. A young man with severe eczema had, against all accepted practice, been immunised against smallpox and later died.

The Significance of a Single Event

In the absence of perspective, information can be dangerous; and nothing is harder to assess than the proper significance of a single dramatic event. Such an event can be greeted by complacency when, in fact, it is the harbinger of disaster; or it causes panic when there is little to worry about. Panic itself can be more dangerous than what gives rise to it. We have, therefore, to control our first reactions by rational thought.

The death of a 14-year-old girl [Natalie Morton in Coventry, England] shortly after immunisation against cervical cancer is certainly a dramatic—and terribly tragic—event. It is increasingly unlikely that the vaccine was responsible for her death: one event following closely upon another is not in itself sufficient proof of causation. But let us, for the sake of argument, accept that the vaccine caused her death. What then?

When the immunisation programme against cervical cancer started, it was estimated, or guessed, that the vaccine might cause one death

Flowers have been placed on the gate of Blue Coat Church of England School in Coventry, England, after the death of student Natalie Morton. Her death was at first attributed to her reaction to a cervical cancer vaccine, but this was later found not to be the cause.

in a million cases: 1.4 million girls have been immunised, and this might be the first death caused by it.

The estimate, or guess, has therefore proved accurate; and if the trials of the vaccine are to be credited, the estimated number of lives eventually saved will far exceed one, and the extra years of life saved will be far in excess of those lost. This is no consolation to the grieving parents, of course; but it is how the rest of us ought to think.

Historical Opposition to Vaccination

Immunisation has always aroused deep hostility, fear and opposition in at least a large part of the population. In England the anti-vaccination movement was a mass phenomenon for more than 70 years from the 1850s to the 1930s, publishing magazines with circulations that today's serious weeklies would envy. Almost every kind of illness was attributed to vaccination by its opponents, including leprosy. When the Government tried to make vaccination compulsory for children in 1858, it eventually had to back down and allow "conscientious objection".

Prominent intellectuals and writers joined the campaign against smallpox vaccination. George Bernard Shaw was a prominent opponent, calling it a delusion. The playwright was a militant ignoramus when it came to matters medical, calling [French microbiologist and chemist Louis] Pasteur and [English surgeon Joseph] Lister charlatans who knew nothing of scientific method. He believed in Dr [Gustav] Jaeger's ludicrous sanitary woollen system, according to which no clothes should be made of vegetable fibre, held by Gustav Jaeger to be the cause of most human ills.

Shaw was himself opposed by Sir Henry Rider Haggard, who had seen the devastation caused by a smallpox epidemic in Africa. In 1898 he wrote a very readable novel in support of vaccination called *Doctor Theme*. The doctor of the title practises in a county

FAST FACT

In September 2009 British teenager Natalie Morton died hours after receiving a cervical cancer vaccine shot, causing panic about the vaccine; but it was later determined that she died from a malignant tumor.

town, where the Liberals ask him to stand for Parliament. This more or less guarantees him election, but he must agree to agitate against vaccination, in which he secretly believes. Ambition gets the better of his belief, but when a smallpox epidemic strikes, he is caught secretly vaccinating himself and is shamed and ruined.

The writer of pulp fiction was, of course, far more intelligent, better informed, honest and interested in the truth of the matter than the great intellectual, who seems to have been motivated mainly by his need for newsworthy contrariness. Shaw, I suspect, would have been mortified by the eradication of smallpox by immunisation, contrary to all he had written over so many years.

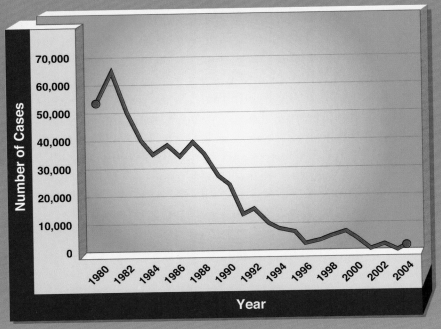

Decline in Global Polio Cases, 1980–2004

Taken from: World Health Organization, "Health Status Statistics: Morbidity; Global Number of Poliomyelitis Cases, 1980–2004."

The Danger of Not Remembering

As common infectious diseases loosen their hold on human beings, so the harms caused by immunisation loom larger and larger in people's minds, obliterating remembrance of conditions before immunisation. Technical improvement is taken for granted the moment it is made (how difficult it is to remember the world before the internet, although many of us have lived most of our lives without it).

Nothing is sooner forgotten than that we have much to be grateful for. Therefore a current death from immunisation counts more than a thousand lives saved by it, in part because a death is tangible but saved life abstract. Conspiracy theories flourish easily on immunisation. It is not difficult to find websites dedicated to the exposure of supposed cover-ups by governments of its alleged harmful effects.

We mistrust the authorities so much in general that their reassurances, even when justified, are disbelieved. Their credit has been so exhausted by past untruths on many matters that we no longer take the trouble to judge properly what is true and what is false: we assume that all is false alike.

Not long ago I reviewed favourably a book about the MMR [measles, mumps, rubella] vaccine controversy by a scholar who took what, in my view, is the correct view that the claims made that it causes autism are false and based on the most obviously deficient scientific research, something that could and should have been obvious from the very first. Indeed, so bad was the science that it should never have been published.

When my review appeared, I was immediately in receipt of abusive letters, not one of which pointed to any fact, but all of which assumed, without any evidence whatsoever (for no such evidence exists), that I was in the pay of the vaccine companies.

Why does immunisation arouse such passions? Are we secretly in love with the diseases that we know, and want them to continue?

EVALUATING THE AUTHORS' ARGUMENTS:

In this viewpoint Theodore Dalrymple claims that the lives saved by vaccines outweigh the lives lost from vaccines. What kind of response might Neil Z. Miller, author of the previous viewpoint, have for Dalrymple on this point?

There May Be a Link Between Vaccines and Autism

Dan Olmsted

In the following viewpoint Dan Olmsted argues that autism is increasing and that the possibility of vaccines as one causal factor has not been appropriately explored. Olmsted claims that there has never been a thorough study of never-vaccinated children in order to see if autism rates are lower in that group. He also claims that the mainstream media has not covered the possible vaccine-autism link with enough scrutiny. Olmsted believes that there is evidence, including possible reactions to a recent four-part vaccine, that autism may be linked with childhood vaccinations. Olmsted argues there is other evidence that autism is caused by environmental pollutants such as mercury, which used to be a common ingredient in vaccines. Olmsted is the managing editor for the blog *Age of Autism* and the coauthor of *The Age of Autism: Mercury, Medicine, and a Man-Made Epidemic*.

"I think autism is soaring due to environmental factors."

"Autism is currently, in our view, the most important and the fastest-evolving disorder in all of medical science and promises to remain so for the foreseeable future," says Dr. Jeffrey A. Lieberman, chairman of the department of psychiatry at Columbia University's school of medicine.

The Issue of Autism

Most mainstream experts believe autism is a genetic disorder that's "increasing" only because of more sophisticated diagnoses. But based on my own reporting, I think autism is soaring due to environmental factors—in the sense of something coming from the outside in—and that genes play a mostly secondary role, perhaps creating a susceptibility to toxic exposures in certain children. As the saying goes: Genes load the gun, environment pulls the trigger.

So to me, the issues autism raises—about the health and well-being of this and future generations, about the role that planetary pollution, chemical inventions and medical interventions may have inadvertently played in triggering it—are so fundamental that by looking at autism, we're looking very deeply into the kind of world we want to inhabit and our children to inherit.

It is impossible to summarize all the issues I've raised in my columns, but to me, four stand out:

The Need to Study Never-Vaccinated Children

The first question I asked when I started looking at autism in late 2004 was this: What is the autism rate among never-vaccinated American children? Vaccines are the leading "environmental" suspect for many families of autistic children. So I was stunned to learn that such a study had never been done, given that it could quickly lay to rest concerns that public health authorities say are dangerously undermining confidence in childhood immunizations.

Rep. Carolyn Maloney, D-N.Y., introduced—and just reintroduced—a bill to force the Department of Health and Human Services to do just that (generously crediting this column for finding enough never-vaccinated children to show that such a study is indeed feasible). She calls it "common sense," and it is an example of ordinary people—through their representatives—telling the experts they want better answers, and fast.

Recently, such a study was in fact done with private funds. It was a $200,000 telephone survey commissioned by the advocacy group Generation Rescue that, as limited as it is scientifically, suggested a disturbing trend: Higher rates of autism in vaccinated vs. never-vaccinated U.S. children, along with similar ratios for other neuro-developmental disorders like attention-deficit/hyperactivity disorder.

I reported the same possible association in the Amish community. That's been criticized as inherently unscientific and undercut by the

New York congresswoman Carolyn Maloney has repeatedly introduced bills that would force the US Department of Health and Human Services to study autism rates in unvaccinated children.

fact that Amish genes may differ from the rest of us and that increasingly, the Amish do receive at least some vaccinations.

All true, but intriguing nonetheless. I also found a family medical practice in Chicago called Homefirst that has thousands of never-vaccinated children as patients. According to its medical director, Mayer Eisenstein, he's aware of only one case of autism and one case of asthma among those kids—not the 1 in 150 and 1 in 10 that are the national averages for those disorders—and he has the medical records to prove it.

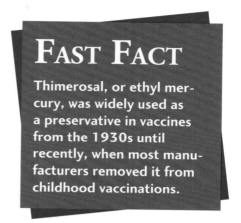

FAST FACT

Thimerosal, or ethyl mercury, was widely used as a preservative in vaccines from the 1930s until recently, when most manufacturers removed it from childhood vaccinations.

I wrote about that in 2005, yet when I met again with Mayer in Chicago last week, he told me not one public health official or medical association has contacted him to express any interest. Nor has any other journalist—not a one.

The Vaccine-Autism Link in the Media

That brings me to my second theme. I am sorry to say my colleagues in the mainstream journalistic community have, in the main, done a lousy job covering this issue. They, of course, would disagree—two were quoted (anonymously!) in the *Columbia Journalism Review* saying, "Olmsted has made up his mind on the question and is reporting the facts that support his conclusions."

Actually, my mind is made up about only one thing: Both vaccinations and autism are so important that definitive, independent research needs to be done yesterday—and the fact that it hasn't should be making more journalists suspicious.

I think Big Media's performance on this issue is on a dismal par with its record leading up to the Iraq war, when for the most part it failed to probe deeply into the intelligence about weapons of mass destruction and the assertions about Saddam Hussein's link to al-Qaida. And it's bad for the same reasons—excessive reliance on "authorities" with obvious conflicts of interest; uncritical enlistment in the "war on terror" and "the war on disease" without considering collateral damage or adverse events; a stenographic and superficial approach to covering the news, and an at-least-semiconscious fear of professional reprisal.

In the case of Iraq, that fear included being cut off—like my exemplary fellow ex-Unipresser [reporter] Helen Thomas—from precious "inside sources" in the government; in the case of autism, fear of alienating advertisers lurks silently in the background.

To see how squeamish and slow-on-the-uptake the media can be in the face of an urgent health crisis, look no further than the early days of AIDS, as chronicled in Randy Shilts' *And the Band Played On* [*: Politics, People, and the AIDS Epidemic*].

The ProQuad Vaccine

Another angle I explored intensively involved a group of families in Olympia, Wash., who noticed their children regressing into autism after getting four live-virus vaccines—mumps, measles, rubella (MMR) and chickenpox—at an early age and in close temporal proximity. These cases seemed to have little or nothing to do with the mercury preservative in other vaccines, called thimerosal, that many parents blame for autism (it was phased out of most routine immunizations starting in 1999).

That raises an ominous prospect: The still-rising autism rate might be related to some other aspect of the immunization schedule as well—timing, age, total load or other ingredients. (I didn't invent that idea; the head of an expert panel mandated by Congress expressed it to me in an interview—and again, her comments were largely ignored.)

One focus of that seven-part Pox series last year [2006] was a case of autism following a small clinical trial of a new vaccine called ProQuad, which contains the live-but-weakened MMR and chickenpox viruses in one shot. The chickenpox virus in ProQuad is about 10 times the amount in the standalone chickenpox shot, a boost needed to overcome "interference" among the four viruses (and a possible sign of trouble right there). Manufacturer Merck says the vaccine is safe and not related to autism.

Earlier this year the company announced it was suspending production of ProQuad—barely a year after its introduction—because supplies of chickenpox vaccine had run unexpectedly low. The company, however, will keep producing its other products containing chickenpox virus: the standalone chickenpox shot and a new vaccine for shingles.

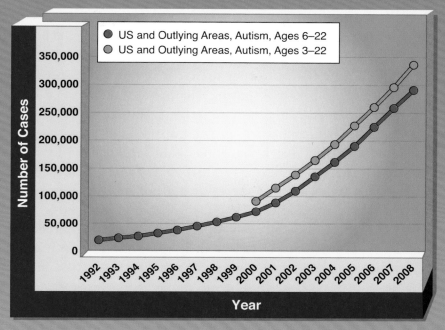

Number of Autism Cases, 1992–2008

● US and Outlying Areas, Autism, Ages 6–22
● US and Outlying Areas, Autism, Ages 3–22

Number of Cases

Year

Taken from: Thoughtful House Center for Children, "Autism: Statistics, Incidence, Prevalence, Rates," 2010.
www.thoughtfulhouse.org/tech-labs/disabilities/autism.php.

A Merck spokesman told me the suspension of ProQuad had nothing to do with any safety concerns, that it had been selling well and would be reintroduced as soon as chickenpox vaccine supplies were replenished. As I've written before, I found Merck to be quite accessible and forthcoming when I asked questions about this issue—much more so than the Food and Drug Administration, in fact.

So I take Merck at its word. But—in the spirit of trust-but-verify—I'll be watching for the return of ProQuad.

The Issue of Mercury

The Age of Autism columns that may mean the most over time are about the first cases of autism, reported in 1943 at Johns Hopkins University in Baltimore among 11 children born in the United States in the 1930s.

With crucial observations from Mark Blaxill of the advocacy group SafeMinds, I've suggested a pattern in some of those early cases:

exposure, through the father's occupation, to ethyl mercury in fungicides. That's the same kind of mercury used in vaccines, and both were introduced commercially around 1930, right when those first autism cases were identified.

This is only a hypothesis, and critics have suggested it is a classic case not of connecting the dots, but of finding what I went looking for. That may be, but put yourself in my place when—more than a year after publicly proposing the mercury fungicide idea in a column—I identified the family of autism's Case 2 and located an extensive archive for the father, a distinguished scientist.

I sat down in the North Carolina State University library and opened the first box, took out the first folder and opened it to the first page. It was a yellowed, typewritten paper from spring 1922 summarizing a fungicide experiment the father conducted as a grad student in plant pathology—an experiment in which mercury was the main ingredient (and in the title). By the time his son was born in 1936, he was working with the new generation of ethyl mercury fungicides—yes, the kind used in vaccines.

Though others will disagree, I find that just a bit outside the parameters of chance, given the timeline of the disorder and the independent belief of so many of today's parents that the same kind of mercury, in a totally different context, triggered their children's autism.

It also suggests that whatever is causing autism could be coming at us from several directions—our increasingly mercury-toxic environment as well as any medical interventions that may be implicated.

EVALUATING THE AUTHOR'S ARGUMENTS:

In this viewpoint Dan Olmsted claims that a study of never-vaccinated children that showed rates of autism similar to rates in vaccinated children could put to rest the worry about an autism-vaccine link. Would a study finding lower rates of autism in never-vaccinated children prove that a link existed? Why or why not?

Viewpoint

4

There Is No Link Between Vaccines and Autism

Claudia Kalb, interview with Alison Singer

"Over and over, the science has shown no causal link between vaccines and autism."

In the following viewpoint Claudia Kalb interviews Alison Singer, a former executive vice-president of communications of Autism Speaks (one of the nation's leading autism advocacy groups). Singer resigned because of a difference of opinion over the need for more research on the safety of vaccines. Singer argues that enough scientific evidence has been presented to show that there is not a causal link between the measles, mumps, and rubella vaccine and autism—or between thimerosal (a vaccine preservative containing mercury) and autism. Singer believes that the money currently spent on vaccine research should be spent on the study of the genetic causes of autism. Kalb, who writes on health, medical, and scientific issues for *Newsweek*, became a senior writer at *Newsweek* in 2004.

AS YOU READ, CONSIDER THE FOLLOWING QUESTIONS:
1. According to Kalb, what does Bob Wright say about vaccine research?
2. According to Singer, how much evidence is there that vaccines do not cause autism?
3. According to Singer, what group is a principal source of funding for autism research?

The warfare over vaccines and autism is heating up yet again. This week, Alison Singer, the executive vice president of communications and awareness at Autism Speaks, one of the nation's leading autism advocacy groups, announced her resignation, citing a difference of opinion over the organization's policy on vaccine research. "Dozens of credible scientific studies have exonerated vaccines as a cause of autism," she wrote in a statement. "I believe we must devote limited funding to more promising avenues of autism research." Singer, who has an 11-year-old daughter with autism, joined the organization when it launched in 2005. Singer praised Autism Speaks and its founders, Bob and Suzanne Wright, but said she could no longer work for a group that supports spending limited resources on vaccine research. Calling Singer's resignation "disappointing and sad," Bob Wright says more authoritative research needs to be conducted on the safety of vaccines given to children under 2. "We all know that autism has genetic causes, but it's highly associated with environmental factors we can't get our hands around," says Wright. "Vaccines fall into that category." *Newsweek*'s Claudia Kalb spoke with Alison Singer about her resignation. Excerpts:

> *Newsweek: Describe Autism Speaks.*

Alison Singer: Autism Speaks is an amazing organization. It has really been a privilege for me to work there. Autism Speaks has raised

FAST FACT

The Centers for Disease Control and Prevention reports that studies continue to show that vaccines are not associated with autism spectrum disorders.

so much awareness of autism and has supported literally thousands of families around the world. I could not be more proud of Autism Speaks and the work that we've done.

But you disagree with their vaccine position?

In general, I disagree with a policy that says, "Despite what this study shows, more studies should be done." At some point, you have to say, "This question has been asked and answered and it's time to move on." We need to be able to say, "Yes, we are now satisfied that the earth is round."

What do you believe the science shows?

There are more than a dozen studies that show no causal link between the MMR [measles-mumps-rubella] vaccine and autism, and thimerosal [a mercury-containing vaccine preservative] and autism. Over and over, the science has shown no causal link between vaccines and autism. My feeling is that if there was an unlimited pot of money at the NIH [National Institutes of Health] from which to fund autism science then it would be fine to say let's study it more. But we don't

A microbiologist is shown doing research at one of the laboratories of the Centers for Disease Control and Prevention (CDC). The CDC has released many studies that show no link between vaccines and autism.

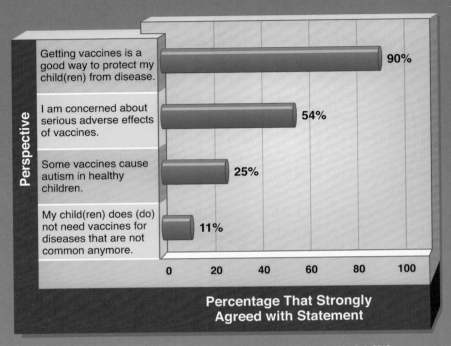

Parental Perspectives on Vaccines

Perspective

- Getting vaccines is a good way to protect my child(ren) from disease. — 90%
- I am concerned about serious adverse effects of vaccines. — 54%
- Some vaccines cause autism in healthy children. — 25%
- My child(ren) does (do) not need vaccines for diseases that are not common anymore. — 11%

(x-axis: 0, 20, 40, 60, 80, 100)

Percentage That Strongly Agreed with Statement

Taken from: Gary L. Freed et al. "Parental Vaccine Safety Concerns in 2009," *Pediatrics*, March 1, 2010.

have that. We have very limited resources and every dollar we spend looking where we know the answer isn't is a dollar we don't have to spend where we might actually find new answers. In general, yes, more research is always better than less. But again, we have limited dollars to spend and we have to use our limited money wisely in ways that are likely to yield new information for families.

How confident are you in the studies that show no vaccine-autism link?

I've read the studies and I've talked to many doctors. One thing that has been a hugely wonderful part of being at Autism Speaks is that I've been able to consult with the top scientists in the field. We work with the top minds. I think that there's this feeling [among some parents] that the vaccine decision is a choice between, "Do I want to risk measles or do I want to risk autism?" That's not a good characterization. We know for a fact that the measles vaccine reduces the risk of getting measles. One choice is backed by science, one choice isn't.

Where would you like to see the research money go?

I think the genetics work has the potential to point us toward important answers. When we can determine which proteins are associated with various genes we can start to understand the mechanism of action that causes autism. Once you understand the mechanism of action, you can start to look for targeted therapies. I would also focus on prenatal exposures. What is a mom exposed to during pregnancy with regard to hormones or maybe medications or even pesticides? Or what's happening in the environment? During flu season, people are more prone to infections so we should look at the incidence of viral infections, flu, hormonal fluctuations and toxins in the environment for both mother and baby.

EVALUATING THE AUTHOR'S ARGUMENTS:

In this viewpoint Claudia Kalb interviews Alison Singer, who accepts the findings of various studies that show no causal link between vaccines and autism, has worked with many doctors in relation to this issue, and has a daughter who has autism. Do these facts influence your response for or against her arguments? Explain.

Viewpoint

5

There Is No Conclusive Evidence That Flu Vaccines Work

Michael Fullerton

"There is virtually no conclusive evidence that flu vaccines are effective at preventing the flu."

In the following viewpoint Michael Fullerton argues that flu vaccines are not as effective as many people think. In fact, Fullerton claims, there is no evidence of a decrease in mortality from flu among those who receive flu vaccinations. He cites several studies that he believes support his view that flu vaccines do not cause decreased mortality from the flu. Fullerton concludes that large-scale randomized placebo-controlled studies are needed to determine conclusively whether flu vaccines work or not. Fullerton is a software developer at CyberMatrix in British Columbia, Canada.

AS YOU READ, CONSIDER THE FOLLOWING QUESTIONS:

1. The author says that some people's reactions to the H1N1 (or swine) flu pandemic consist largely of what two extreme points of view?

2. What does the author say happened to flu mortality rates when, in 2004, there was a drop in the rates of production of flu vaccine?

3. In what two years does the author claim that the wrong flu vaccine was distributed without an increase in mortality?

It is quite troubling to witness the hysterical reactions to the H1N1 "pandemic." Some are more than ready to roll up their sleeves for a largely untested vaccine containing frightening ingredients like mercury, formaldehyde and squalene. Some even fear the vaccine is a plot to cull the human herd by 80%. As usual the truth lies somewhere in the middle of these extremes of misplaced trust and paranoia. Let me lay down the cold hard scientific truth for you in the least boring way I can muster. The idea behind vaccines seems straightforward enough. When you get the flu your body produces antibodies to fight it. So if a dead flu virus is injected into your body, your body's immune system will produce antibodies to it without you getting sick and you won't get that strain of flu later on. The problem is that those with impaired immune systems, those that need the vaccine the most, do not respond well to vaccines because, well, their immune systems don't work as well. People with strong immune systems, on the other hand, will be able to fight off the flu themselves without needing a vaccine. Surely this simplistic common sense approach is refuted by the massive scientific support for flu vaccine effectiveness.

> **FAST FACT**
>
> In June 2009 the World Health Organization declared a new strain of swine-origin Influenza A H1N1 virus to be a pandemic.

The Ineffectiveness of Flu Vaccines

The sad fact though, is that there is virtually no conclusive evidence that flu vaccines are effective at preventing the flu. A recent article in the magazine, *The Atlantic* explains why. The belief that flu vaccines are

THE SYMPTOMS ARE UNMISTAKEABLE:

FIRST COMES A VAGUE SENSE OF NAUSEA...

...FOLLOWED BY PROFUSE SWEATING...

...THEN TREMBLING...

...AND SHORTNESS OF BREATH.

IT'S FEAR SEASON, AGAIN.

THE FLU IS BACK!! THERE'S NOT ENOUGH VACCINE! WE'RE ALL GONNA DIE!

effective comes from cohort studies. These cohort studies examine the death rates in large groups of people that choose to get vaccinated with death rates in groups that don't. The problem is that cohort studies are extremely susceptible to bias. Confounding factors like education, lifestyle and income can influence the results in a major way. In 2006 Dr. Lisa Jackson published a study in *International Journal of Epidemiology* to test her hypothesis that those who choose to get vaccinated tend to be younger and healthier. Her study showed that outside the flu season, people that don't get vaccinated still have a 60% higher death rate over those that do. This study clearly shows that confounding factors explain the mortality differences and not vaccine effectiveness. In other words, there is no evidence then that flu vaccines do anything but increase the profits of mega pharmaceutical companies.

The Atlantic article also notes that in 2004 there was a 40% drop in flu vaccine production rates, yet mortality rates did not increase. In 1968 and 1997 the wrong flu vaccine was distributed and again there was no mortality increase. Dr. Sumit Majumdar of the University of Alberta notes that despite the dramatic increase in vaccination rates of the elderly there has been no decline in mortality rates. The Cochrane Collaboration's Tom Jefferson has extensively examined all flu vaccine studies and notes that almost all these studies were deeply flawed. Of the only four studies he found to be properly designed, only two showed any benefit and only in certain groups such as school children with no underlying health issues. As Jefferson rightly explains, the only way to conclusively determine if flu vaccines work is to perform

People in Idaho line up to get the H1N1 vaccine. The vaccine has come under criticism for being released largely untested.

large scale randomized placebo-controlled trial studies. Such studies involve randomly giving half the test subjects vaccine and the other half a placebo. The usual hysterical reaction to this is that it would be highly unethical to conclusively prove a treatment works because you would deny the treatment to those that need it. Unethical? Basing large scale health initiatives on highly unsound pseudo-science and circular logic is monstrously unethical. Clearly in the business of politics rational objectivity, sound science and ethics mean little.

EVALUATING THE AUTHOR'S ARGUMENTS:

In this viewpoint Michael Fullerton argues that the only way to determine whether flu vaccines work is to perform large-scale randomized placebo-controlled studies, but he notes that such studies are resisted, based on the view that they are unethical. What assumption about flu vaccines underlies the view that doing such studies is unethical?

Viewpoint 6

Flu Vaccines Are Safe and Vital for Public Health

"The vaccinations are safe, they are effective and they build a wall of protection for you and your community."

Milwaukee Journal Sentinel

In the following viewpoint the *Milwaukee Journal Sentinel* argues that flu vaccines, and in particular the vaccine for the 2009 outbreak of the swine flu, are safe and effective. The swine flu, or H1N1, is a particularly virulent flu virus, and people need to be vaccinated, the author argues. The *Journal Sentinel* claims there is far too much misinformation and skepticism about the swine flu vaccine. The *Journal Sentinel* also addresses what it believes to be four myths about the swine flu vaccine and urges people to get vaccinated to protect themselves. The *Milwaukee Journal Sentinel* is a newspaper in Milwaukee, Wisconsin.

AS YOU READ, CONSIDER THE FOLLOWING QUESTIONS:

1. The author cites a study that claims that what fraction of people hospitalized with swine flu end up in intensive care?
2. According to the author, what percentage of those surveyed by the University of Michigan were inclined not to vaccinate their children for the swine flu?
3. One out of how many Americans dies each year from swine flu, according to the author?

orget about Bill Maher and Glenn Beck. Go get a flu shot—especially if you belong to a group most at risk for the disease. The vaccinations are safe, they are effective and they build a wall of protection for you and your community.

The 2009 Swine Flu

Maher, a left-wing comedian, wrote on Twitter recently: "If u get a swine flu shot ur an idiot."

Beck, a conservative talk show host for Fox News, raised the possibility that the neurological disease Guillain-Barré Syndrome would break out. "How much do you trust your government?" Beck asked. "I think that's the main question."

Think about it for a moment. Glenn Beck? Bill Maher? Or the best scientists in the country?

We'll go with the scientists. They believe the swine flu vaccine is safe. They believe Americans who are most at risk should receive it.

The swine flu—H1N1—has spread to 191 countries and infected millions of people, killing more than 4,500. Because the outbreak of disease last spring [2009] seemed so mild, a false sense of security seems to have fallen over Milwaukee and the rest of the country. It would be a mistake to underestimate the killing power of H1N1.

FAST FACT

The Centers for Disease Control and Prevention estimates that between 43 million and 89 million cases of 2009 H1N1 flu occurred between April 2009 and April 2010.

A recent study by the *New England Journal of Medicine* found that most people who get H1N1 are sick for several days and recover on their own. But for those who require hospitalization, the outlook is much worse: One in four ended up in intensive care, and 7% died. The swine flu is most prevalent in children, young adults and pregnant women. At the moment [October 2009], about 99% of all flu diagnosed in Wisconsin is H1N1.

The government hopes to vaccinate pregnant women, health care workers, children with underlying health conditions between the ages of 6 months and 24 years and older Americans with underlying

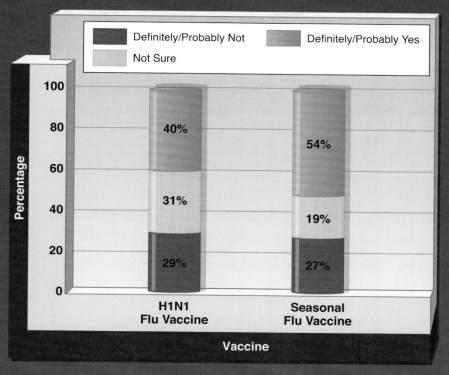

Parents' Plans to Have Children Get H1N1 and Seasonal Flu Vaccine

Legend: Definitely/Probably Not · Not Sure · Definitely/Probably Yes

H1N1 Flu Vaccine: 40% · 31% · 29%

Seasonal Flu Vaccine: 54% · 19% · 27%

Y-axis: Percentage (0, 20, 40, 60, 80, 100)
X-axis: Vaccine

Taken from: C.S. Mott Children's Hospital National Poll on Children's Health, 2009.

health conditions. Ideally, about half the population would receive the vaccine.

Misinformation and Skepticism

However, a contagion of misinformation is causing needless hesitation. Sixty percent of those surveyed in a recent University of Michigan poll said they either wouldn't vaccinate their children against the swine flu or weren't sure if they would. A *Consumer Reports* survey found similar sentiments.

So much skepticism about such a common-sense act of public health is astonishing. Vaccination is a front-line defense against disease. Children have been vaccinated for years against deadly diseases such as diphtheria and whooping cough with few side effects and have been spared suffering and death. If large numbers of people forgo vaccination and the disease becomes more virulent, hospitals could be overwhelmed.

And it's not just funny guys and TV gabbers peddling bad advice. Smart people who should know better are using the Internet's echo chamber to do the same. The popular medical website Mercola.com recently listed nine reasons you shouldn't vaccinate your kids against swine flu. Among them is the implication, without a shred of evidence, that vaccinations cause autism. The science is rock solid on this:

No study has ever found such a link.

"We're fighting two wars—a virus that can mutate—but we're also fighting something that is bigger than that. And that is fear," Milwaukee Health Commissioner Bevan Baker said.

Myths About the H1N1 Vaccine

The myth makers are working hard, so we'll have to work harder:

Myth: The vaccine was rushed into production; it wasn't properly tested.
Reality: In clinical trials, the National Institutes of Health and makers of the vaccine have proved that it is safe. The U.S. Food and Drug Administration has licensed it. Secretary of Health and Human Services Kathleen Sebelius says the vaccine "has been made exactly the same way seasonal flu vaccine has been made, year in and year out."

Myth: Flu shots cause serious side effects including death.
Reality: Every year, tragedy strikes people around the time they get their flu shots—a person gets a flu shot and suffers a heart attack or other life-threatening ailment. This is coincidence. The Centers for Disease Control and Prevention has received no reports of serious side effects from the swine flu vaccine. The same people who got the vaccination and became ill probably used their cell phones the day they were stricken. It would be just as logical to blame their ring tones.

Myth: The federal government is requiring everyone to get the vaccination.
Reality: Wrong. It's voluntary.

Myth: A lot of people came down with Guillain-Barré Syndrome in 1976 after President Gerald Ford ordered everyone to get a swine flu vaccination.
Reality: A scientific review by the federal Institute of Medicine in 2003 concluded that people who received the swine flu vaccine in 1976 had a slightly increased risk for developing the neurological ailment, Guillain-Barré. Since then, numerous studies have found no association between later flu vaccines and the disease, although two studies suggested that about one additional person for every million receiving the seasonal flu vaccine may be at some increased risk for the syndrome.

President Barack Obama receives the H1N1 vaccine. His participation helped diffuse some of the hysteria surrounding the usefulness of the vaccine.

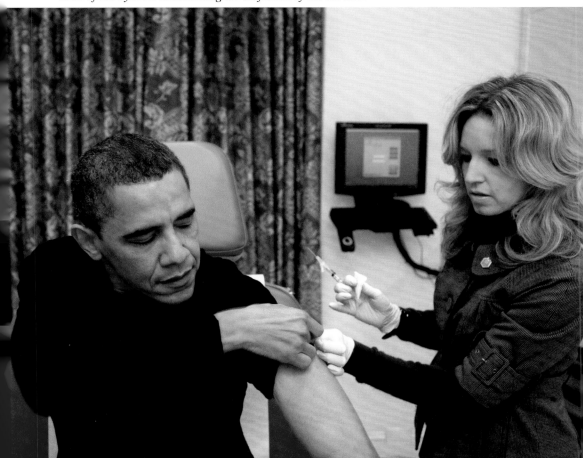

Guillain-Barré causes the body to attack its own nerve cells, resulting in weakness, occasionally paralysis and, rarely, death. Each week in the United States, about 140 new cases are diagnosed, leading some to speculate that coincidence may have played a role 33 years ago.

But the odds of dying from the flu are far worse than the odds of contracting Guillain-Barré. Each year, 1 in 8,400 Americans die from seasonal influenza.

The vast majority of people who get flu shots tolerate them well and have few, if any, side effects. The swine flu vaccine has been thoroughly tested; the government says it is safe.

The community benefit is just as important as the individual protection the vaccine provides. If you are vaccinated, you will not spread the disease to other people. One person at a time, a wall of protection can be built in the community to prevent needless deaths.

"There is nothing scarier than seeing a 10-year-old on a respirator," Baker said. "Seventeen kids died in the last 10 days in the United States. There is nothing scarier than that."

Get that vaccination.

EVALUATING THE AUTHORS' ARGUMENTS:

In this viewpoint the *Milwaukee Journal Sentinel* argues that many people die from the flu each year. Given what Michael Fullerton, author of the previous viewpoint, says about the flu vaccine, would that number go up, down, or stay the same without a flu vaccine?

Chapter 2

Should Vaccinations Be Mandatory?

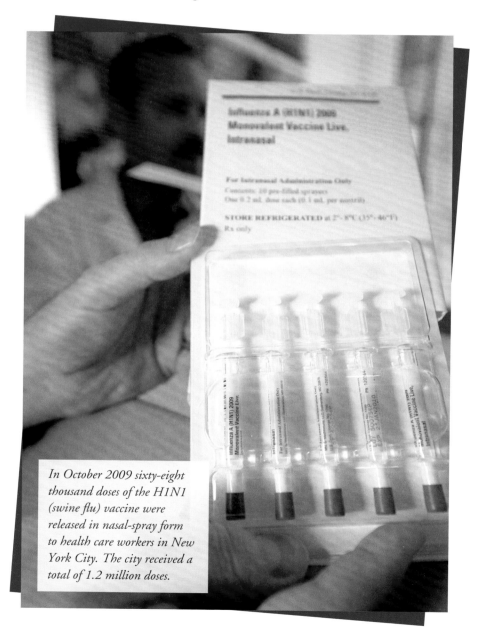

In October 2009 sixty-eight thousand doses of the H1N1 (swine flu) vaccine were released in nasal-spray form to health care workers in New York City. The city received a total of 1.2 million doses.

Parents Need to Follow Mandatory Vaccination Requirements

Mike King

"States should not back off mandatory vaccination laws, and local school districts and health departments should do a better job of enforcing compliance."

In the following viewpoint Mike King contends that a recent increase in measles is due to parents who do not follow mandatory vaccination laws. King claims that parents who willfully choose not to vaccinate often do so out of unfounded fears about the risks of vaccination. King argues that schools and public authorities need to do a better job of enforcing the law by requiring parents to vaccinate their children, especially if they are going to attend public school, where diseases spread easily. King was an editorial columnist for the *Atlanta Journal-Constitution* until his retirement in 2008.

AS YOU READ, CONSIDER THE FOLLOWING QUESTIONS:

1. According to the author, in the first half of 2008 how many children were sickened with measles?
2. What two possible explanations does the author give for the rise of autism in recent years?
3. King claims that each year how many children aged six months to five years die of influenza?

Unfounded fears about vaccines are causing too many parents to forgo getting the shots their children need to stay healthy and not spread dangerous diseases among their playmates.

A Decline in Vaccinations

The Centers for Disease Control and Prevention [CDC] said last month that measles cases in the United States had reached the highest level in more than a decade, an alarming rise in a disease thought to be eliminated in the United States eight years ago. The spike is directly linked to parents refusing to get their children inoculated against the easily spread disease.

In the first six months of the year [2008] measles outbreaks have sickened 131 children in 15 states, sending more than a dozen youngsters to the hospital for treatment. Virtually all of the children were home-schooled, the CDC said, and thus had no proof of their immunization status as would be required in public schools.

> **FAST FACT**
>
> According to the Centers for Disease Control and Prevention, more than one in four children are not in compliance with official vaccination recommendations.

Even in public schools, those requirements are too often ignored. According to a Spotlight report in Sunday's [October 26, 2008] *Atlanta Journal-Constitution*, many metro Atlanta school districts and health departments do not require immunization proof when children are enrolled. Reporter Alison Young found that 99 elementary schools and 81 middle schools in metro Atlanta failed to meet the

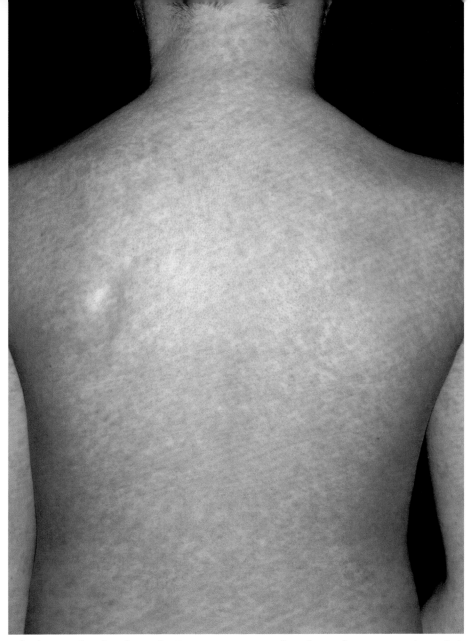

This boy is infected with measles. Because some parents have been reluctant to vaccinate their children, measles cases have reached their highest level in a decade.

state's minimum requirement that 90 percent of their students have vaccination records showing they are up-to-date on the shots needed to prevent the spread of communicable childhood diseases. Fewer than half of students in some Atlanta and Fulton County schools have proof of proper vaccinations.

Parents fail to get their children inoculated for a variety of reasons: ignorance of the requirement; concern over how much it will cost; misunderstanding that for the vaccine to be effective against some diseases, children must get follow-up shots. But public health departments will provide information as well as the vaccines for any child, regardless of ability to pay.

Parents' Unfounded Fears About Vaccines

More problematic are the parents who willfully ignore the requirement, substituting their judgment for that of experts who must guard the public health. In New Jersey, the state Legislature is being asked to approve a bill that would allow parents to opt out of mandatory vaccine requirements [the bill never became law]. The measure was prompted by a new requirement in New Jersey—the first in the nation—that pre-schoolers get annual flu shots.

The parental blow-back on vaccines began a decade ago when a study purportedly showed that a mercury-based preservative in the measles, mumps and rubella (MMR) vaccine was in some way linked to a group of autistic children who had developed gastrointestinal problems. The preservative was removed from the manufacturing process for vaccines, and numerous, large and well-documented scientific studies since then have failed to show any evidence of a link to autism. Earlier this year, scientists also tried but failed to replicate the original 1998 study allegedly linking vaccines and autism.

Nevertheless, fears about tainted vaccines are still pervasive on the Internet, where parents are subjected to heart-rendering anecdotal stories about unexplained autism in children. A handful of celebrity parents of autistic children have also raised the issue and garnered disproportionate attention to the cause.

Unfortunately, there is no clear explanation why the rate of autism has risen in recent years. Many scientists believe it is the result of more vigilant observation among parents and pediatricians and earlier testing among children. Others point out that the range of symptoms defined as autism—both behavioral and physical—has greatly expanded, which in turn has resulted in more children being diagnosed with the condition or some variation of it.

However, the anti-vaccine crowd's call for "caution" in allowing parents to decide for themselves whether their children should be inoculated is risky business. Certainly, public health authorities should have the ability to require vaccines for children attending public schools, which serve as the primary vector for disease outbreaks.

The Need to Enforce Mandatory Vaccination

The influenza vaccine debate in New Jersey offers an example. The CDC and public health experts have recommended in recent years that yearly flu shots be given to all children six months to 5 years of age. That means that pre-schoolers and children in daycare should be getting it, which is what prompted New Jersey's requirement.

Each year, some 20,000 children in that age group are stricken with influenza; about 100 of them die. The flu generally strikes earlier and harder in children, whose immune systems are weaker than those of adults. Young children also are much more likely to spread the virus to their family, teachers and caregivers. If the disease is suppressed in children, it will not gain a foothold and likely decline among adults as well.

New Jersey, like Georgia and most other states, already allows children to be exempted from vaccine requirements if their parents have religious objections or if there is a legitimate medical reason. The bill in the New Jersey Legislature would allow parents a "conscientious exemption" as long as they swear they have "sincerely held" objections to immunizations.

No doubt many parents have sincerely held beliefs, but allowing them to opt out of vaccination puts the lives of their children at risk as well as the lives of others.

Vaccinations for infectious childhood diseases are one of the greatest accomplishments of medical science, saving millions of lives annually. But their effectiveness is directly linked to coverage that is as universal as possible.

The vaccine-autism link has been thoroughly debunked. States should not back off mandatory vaccination laws, and local school districts and health departments should do a better job of enforcing compliance.

Parents' Freedom of Conscience Applies to Vaccination

Peggy O'Mara

> "Parents are the only ones who will live with the consequences of their actions, so they must be the ones who make the final decisions."

In the following viewpoint Peggy O'Mara argues that parents' freedom of conscience is protected by the US Constitution, allowing them to make a broad range of choices about their children, including deciding whether to have them vaccinated. She claims that parents who make choices contrary to the majority, such as parents who choose not to vaccinate, are vilified unfairly in the media. O'Mara concludes that parents should continue to exercise their freedom to make choices about their children in spite of the growing intolerance for their views. O'Mara is the publisher, editor, and owner of *Mothering* magazine and the author of *Natural Family Living: The* Mothering Magazine *Guide to Parenting*.

AS YOU READ, CONSIDER THE FOLLOWING QUESTIONS:
1. O'Mara claims that based on current measles incidence levels, a death from measles occurs how often?
2. From where, according to the Centers for Disease Control and Prevention, do most new measles cases originate?
3. The author argues that intolerance for parents' freedom of conscience is breeding what?

As the editor of *Mothering* [magazine], I see circumcision and vaccination as two of many issues that fall under the broader umbrella of informed consent or freedom of conscience. Sometimes people will characterize the magazine as pro-homebirth or anti-vaccine because of our frequent coverage of these issues. In fact, we are pro–informed consent; we publish both sides of the story so that parents can be aware of all angles before they make a decision. It was in this spirit of informed consent that I first became interested in covering HIV and AIDS. In 1996, I received a letter from Michael Eliner of Health, Education, AIDS Liaison (HEAL) in New York City. Michael asked *Mothering* to look into the new recommendation that all mothers and newborns be tested for HIV. In the Summer 1997 issue of *Mothering*, I reported that universal HIV testing, like universal prenatal testing, is controversial because AIDS is rare among women of childbearing age and among newborns.

Parents' Freedom of Conscience

Not only is universal HIV testing for pregnant women and newborns controversial, but also are the medications prescribed for HIV and the recommendations regarding breastfeeding. . . .

The choices facing mothers who question mandatory medication for HIV are not unlike those faced by parents who choose to give birth at home in a country where 99 percent of births take place in the hospital, or parents who decide not to circumcise their son, even though the majority of their peers are doing so. These choices are not unlike those made by parents who wonder if they can delay childhood vaccines, select some but not all of them, or forego them altogether.

These parents exercise their freedom of conscience—a right supported by US courts for more than 100 years. Freedom of conscience is protected under the doctrine of informed consent, which specifically protects the right to decline. For informed consent to be valid, a decision must not be coerced.

Advocates of freedom of conscience say parents have the right to choose whether to vaccinate their children.

Parents' freedom of conscience has been demonized of late. A new book, *Autism's False Prophets: Bad Science, Risky Medicine, and the Search for a Cure* by Paul A. Offit, MD, patronizes suffering parents of autistic children and dismisses them as part of a hysterical conspiracy of alarmists. The tragic death of John Travolta and Kelly Preston's son was cruelly sensationalized by suggestions that perhaps the Scientologist couple hadn't done enough to care for their son, who, in fact, had 24/7 supervision. On October 28, 2008, in its fifth episode of the season, the television show *Law & Order: Special Victims Unit* vilified Christine Maggiore, one of the mothers featured in our September 1998 article, in which a daughter and mother both die of AIDS.

> **FAST FACT**
>
> According to a 2009 study published in the journal *Pediatrics*, 31 percent of parents believe they should have the right to refuse vaccines for their children for any reason.

The Media Portrayal of Non-vaccinators

On January 8, 2009, the television show *Private Practice* aired an episode about a child who brings measles into a medical clinic and the widespread panic that ensues. Parents who don't vaccinate are called child abusers and portrayed as pariahs. Measles is depicted as a life-threatening disease instead of the mild illness that my friends and I all had as children. In the *Private Practice* episode, the child dies from measles, an occurrence that is so rare that, based on the current incidence levels (42 in 2007), a death from measles would happen once every 119 years. Even if the incidence of measles were to quadruple, we would not see a death for 30 years. The current death rate from measles is 1 in 5,000, yet it is portrayed in the show as though it happens frequently.

In this episode, a doctor forcibly vaccinates the sick child's brother for measles as his mother stands by protesting helplessly. While the actors who play the doctors in the show are all ridiculously good-looking and remarkably fit, the non-vaccinators appear dowdy and dangerous. One wears no makeup, is slightly overweight, and

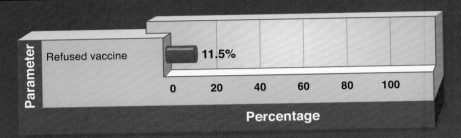

Have you refused a vaccine for your child(ren) that a doctor recommended?

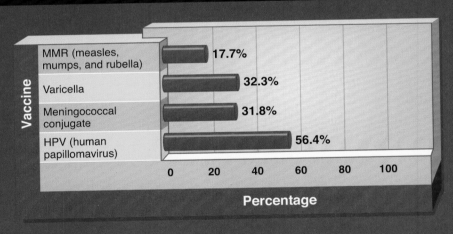

Of those who have refused any vaccines, the following specific vaccines were refused:

Taken from: Gary L. Freed et al. "Parental Vaccine Safety Concerns in 2009," *Pediatrics*, March 1, 2010.

occasionally hysterical. The other is a sometimes drug addict who forgets to vaccinate.

The incidence of measles cases has risen dramatically from 2007 to 2008 and is at its highest level in more than a decade. According to the Centers for Disease Control and Prevention (CDC), 63 of the 131 new cases of measles from January to July 2008 were among those unvaccinated. The majority of the cases (68), however, were among those vaccinated. Interestingly, according to the CDC, 89 percent of the 131 new measles cases were "imported from or associated with importations from other countries, particularly countries in Europe, where several outbreaks are ongoing." In the face of this evidence, why is it the conscientious objectors who are scapegoated? The growing propaganda that unvaccinated kids put vaccinated kids at risk is not supported by the evidence and just doesn't make sense as long as the vaccines themselves are effective.

An Intolerance for Parental Choice

Now even parents who sleep with their babies are being portrayed as dangerous kooks. On January 25, 2009, our local paper, the *Santa Fe New Mexican*, reprinted on the front page an article from the *Washington Post* titled, "Infant Deaths Rekindle Bed-Share Debate." The article reports on a study to be published in the February 2009 issue of the journal *Pediatrics*, showing an increase in deaths attributed to accidental suffocation and strangulation in bed (ASSB) from 2.8 to 12.5 per 100,000 between 1984 and 2004. . . .

The *Pediatrics* research was based on epidemiological analysis of infant mortality data. Without a detailed death-scene investigation, an autopsy, and a review of the medical records, it is doubtful that infant deaths are correctly classified on death certificates. Even when there is an autopsy, it is impossible to tell the difference between a death from strangulation and a death from a physiological cause, such as a heart defect.

A dangerously vicious intolerance for parents' freedom of conscience is growing and is breeding an atmosphere of distrust among families. It's especially important now for parents to clearly differentiate between the personal and the political. If you exercise your freedom of conscience and make a decision that is held by only a small minority, be reassured by the knowledge that the Constitution of the United States was written specifically to protect minority opinions. If you have made a responsible and well-informed decision, you can dismiss the propaganda when an issue is demonized in the press, because its coverage may be influenced by political, that is, financial, motives. Parents are the only ones who will live with the consequences of their actions, so they must be the ones who make the final decisions. Anything else is tyranny.

EVALUATING THE AUTHORS' ARGUMENTS:

In this viewpoint Peggy O'Mara argues that parents should be allowed to make decisions about issues such as vaccination because they "are the only ones who will live with the consequences of their actions." How might Mike King, author of the previous viewpoint, disagree with O'Mara on this point?

Health Care Workers Should Get the Flu Vaccine

Buffalo News

> *"The precedent for mandatory shots already is established."*

In the following viewpoint the *Buffalo News* argues that New York State's mandate that all health care professionals receive the H1N1 (swine flu) vaccine should be followed. The newspaper contends that health care workers are uniquely situated to come into contact with many high-risk populations, justifying the vaccine mandate. The *Buffalo News* claims that resistance by health care professionals to the mandate harms the public policy push to achieve widespread vaccination in the general public and concludes that health care workers should comply with the mandate to help in preventing flu epidemics. The *Buffalo News* is a newspaper in Buffalo, New York.

AS YOU READ, CONSIDER THE FOLLOWING QUESTIONS:

1. According to the author, what fact about health care jobs puts workers at a greater risk of exposure to swine flu?
2. Every state already requires health care workers to be immunized against what three diseases, according to the author?
3. What is the author's advice to health care workers resistant to the mandatory vaccination requirement?

The debate about whether New York should be forcing health professionals to take the swine flu vaccine is really two questions.

Vaccines and the Health Care Profession

Question 1: Should health professionals take the vaccine? The answer is yes, of course they should.

Question 2: Should the state Health Department be requiring all hospital, home health and hospice workers to get seasonal and swine flu vaccines on pain of dismissal? The answer is, good question, but while we're debating it, refer to Question 1.

Anyone can be exposed to the swine flu virus, of course, and anyone who deals with large numbers of people—teachers, toll-booth staffers and ticket-takers at Ralph Wilson Stadium, for example—may be at heightened risk. But health care providers fall into a special category, and for a couple of reasons.

First of all, their jobs require them to come into contact with sick people all day long. That puts them at greater risk of exposure than most other professions. That leads to the second reason, which is that a sick health care professional can pass along the virus to patients, who are liable to include high-risk populations, including the elderly and those with weakened immune systems.

> **FAST FACT**
>
> In October 2009 New York governor David A. Patterson halted enforcement of the state regulation that health care workers be vaccinated for H1N1, due to vaccine scarcity.

Resistance to the H1N1 Flu Shot

Some of the resistance to taking the vaccine is tied to the false belief that this is a new, insufficiently tested vaccine that could have unknown side effects. But the fact is that the H1N1 flu shot is simply a variation on the seasonal flu shots that have been used for years. A typical flu season results in some 36,000 deaths, while there have been no known deaths from the vaccines.

What is more, every state already requires health workers to be immunized against measles, mumps and polio. The unions, which are protesting the swine-flu mandate, make no complaints about those other immunizations. The precedent for mandatory shots already is established.

It is easy to understand the skittishness that arises when the government requires that anyone take something into his or her body,

Health care workers at the Wishard Memorial Hospital in Indianapolis were the first health care workers in the nation to be vaccinated against swine flu.

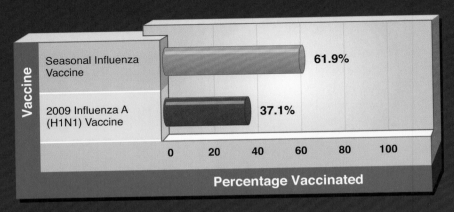

Taken from: *Morbidity and Mortality Weekly Report*, "Interim Results: Influenza A (H1N1) 2009 Monovalent and Seasonal Influenza Vaccination Coverage Among Health-Care Personnel—United States, August 2009–January 2010," vol. 59, no.12, April 2, 2010, pp. 357-62. www.cdc.gov/mmwr/preview/mmwrhtml/mm5912a1.htm.

especially when it is a sort-of-new product for a new flu. New York, thus far, is the only state to require this immunization of health care workers. Does that put it out of step or in the lead? Whichever you believe, it's a defensible requirement as the state and nation prepare for a potentially virulent flu season. And if health care professionals truly believe widespread vaccination is the best way to prevent an epidemic, then the balking of professionals already has damaged efforts to get the public to participate.

Take the Shot

No doubt, the argument will continue. Nobody likes being told what to do, especially by the government. Still, our advice to resistant health care workers is to continue the mandatory-policy debate, but take the shot. Pretend it's your own idea if you have to.

In that way, health care workers can do the smart and safe thing—protecting themselves and their patients—while also obeying the rules, keeping their jobs and giving the controversy over the policy issue time to sort itself out. We'll know soon enough if the requirement made a difference in transmission of this virus. Then we'll know better if the requirement is necessary.

Viewpoint
4

The Flu Vaccine Should Not Be Mandatory for Health Care Workers

New York State Nurses Association

"The Nurses Association questions the authority of this body to impose such a sweeping mandate as an emergency rule, without the declaration of a public health emergency."

In the following viewpoint by the New York State Nurses Association (NYSNA), the association contends that mandating that health care workers be vaccinated for the flu is unwarranted. Such a mandate, the NYSNA argues, is not the best way to prevent the transmission of flu since the vaccine is not always effective, and other important components of an effective flu-prevention program may be ignored if vaccinations become mandatory. The NYSNA argues that a voluntary immunization program can work well, whereas a mandatory program could cause nurses to leave the profession. The thirty-six-thousand-member New York State Nurses Association is the oldest and largest state professional association for registered nurses in the United States.

New York State Nurses Association (NYSNA), testimony delivered to the State Hospital Review and Planning Council Codes and Regulations Committee, New York, NY, July 23, 2009. Copyright © 2009 NYSNA. Reproduced by permission. www.nysna.org.

1. According to the author, what is an important difference between the flu vaccine and vaccines for measles and rubella?
2. According to the New York State Nurses Association, influenza is transmitted in what three ways?
3. The New York State Nurses Association is concerned that the New York flu vaccine mandate for health workers has no provision allowing an exemption for what two reasons?

While the association [New York State Nurses Association] agrees that nurses and other healthcare providers should be immunized for seasonal influenza, it does not agree that nurses should be required to be immunized as a condition of employment.

The Efficacy of Mandatory Vaccination

The state currently requires that healthcare workers be immunized for measles and rubella, diseases that can be eradicated by one or two immunizations in a lifetime. We have seen the benefit to the public by the virtual elimination of measles, mumps, rubella, smallpox, and polio.

Influenza, however, cannot be eradicated. It is a constantly mutating virus and the flu vaccine must be administered annually. If this proposal takes effect, nurses will have to submit to vaccinations every year for the remainder of their careers in order to continue working or to get jobs in direct patient care. And will this really ensure patient safety or prevent the spread of a flu virus?

The seasonal flu vaccine is not 100% effective and sometimes is highly ineffective, as it was in 2005 and again in 2007. There is no guarantee that in any given year, the public will benefit from mandatory immunization of healthcare providers.

As I said, the Nurses Association encourages nurses to voluntarily get flu shots. We question whether the Department of Health [DOH] and healthcare facilities have devoted sufficient time and resources to promoting voluntary immunization. Successful programs include educational components that target specific objections, offer the vaccine

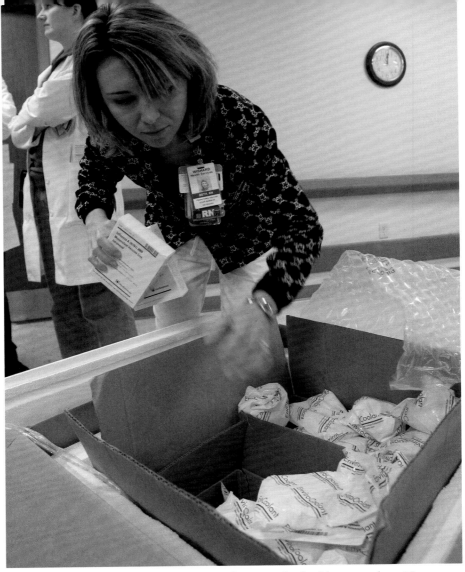

A nurse pulls swine flu vaccine that will be administered to health care workers. Many nurses think the vaccination program should be voluntary, rather than mandatory.

at no cost at a time and place convenient for workers, and employ other strategies that have been proven to work. In June 2009, the Joint Commission issued a monograph with 28 examples of hospitals that have improved their immunization rates.

An Effective Prevention Program

Immunizations are only part of an overall strategy to prevent the spread of influenza virus. When novel H1N1 influenza appeared this spring [2009], nurses were concerned about taking the proper infection control measures when caring for suspected H1N1 cases. When the Nurses Association evaluated the readiness of hospitals to deal with a possible public health emergency, we were shocked to discover that many facilities were unprepared.

Influenza is transmitted three ways: droplet (between 5 and 10 microns), airborne aerosol (less than 5 microns), and contact. There is evidence that at least some infection is spread through the airborne route. In its Standard 29 CFR 1910.134, the Occupational Safety and Health Administration (OSHA) requires that healthcare workers be given properly fitted N-95 respirators to protect against airborne infection. But, in New York State, some hospitals did not have enough N-95 respirators available and had not performed the necessary fit testing. Some had not performed the OSHA-required risk assessment process.

Is it possible that the DOH and healthcare facilities see mandatory immunizations as an "easy fix" that promises to prevent workers from contracting both seasonal flu and H1N1? By providing flu shots, will hospitals be able to avoid establishing and implementing effective infection control policies and procedures? What strategy does DOH have to ensure that federally mandated infection control procedures are being followed?

FAST FACT

A New York judge issued a temporary restraining order to prevent the state from enforcing the controversial mandatory flu vaccination, days before it was suspended by the governor for reasons of vaccine scarcity.

All recommendations from OSHA, the Centers for Disease Control and Prevention, and other epidemiology and workplace safety organizations emphasize the "risk" to healthcare workers for contracting and spreading the flu virus. None propose mandatory immunization, by the way.

Recommendations for preventing the spread of infection are based on hazard assessment and determining the risk to workers from the identified hazards. The proposed regulations ignore the risk assessment process, but rather apply a "scorched earth" approach. Ignoring

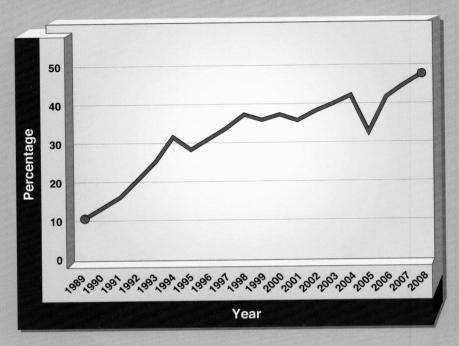

Percentage of Health Care Workers Vaccinated Against Influenza

Taken from: National Health Interview Survey, 1989–2008.

hazard assessment misses the key information needed to create a truly effective prevention program.

An Unjustified Mandate

The Nurses Association questions the authority of this body to impose such a sweeping mandate as an emergency rule, without the declaration of a public health emergency. When there is a public health emergency and the governor or state health official initiates a public health strategy to curb the spread of a communicable disease, the state may mandate quarantine, vaccine, or other such measures for the public good. But the action must have a real and substantial relation to an immediate threat to the public health and safety.

We are concerned that nurses would be exempted from the proposed mandate only if the influenza immunization is medically contraindicated. The proposed regulations have no provision for religious or cultural preferences regarding immunization, effectively blocking individuals who have these beliefs from earning their livelihood. It's possible that nurses will leave the profession or choose another career because of this onerous mandate; a serious threat at a time when the shortage of nurses in New York State is expected to reach 20,000 within a decade.

EVALUATING THE AUTHORS' ARGUMENTS:

In this viewpoint the New York State Nurses Association claims that the flu vaccine is not 100 percent effective. Do you think the author of the previous viewpoint, the *Buffalo News,* would find this to be a good argument against a vaccination mandate for health workers? Why or why not?

Whether to Get the H1N1 Vaccine Is a Personal Decision

Leslie Donald

"I definitely have my opinions on vaccinations; however, I have always felt that it is a very personal decision that should be made by an informed person."

In the following viewpoint Leslie Donald argues that whether to get vaccinated is a decision that needs to be made on a personal level after exploring the information for and against the vaccination. In the case of the swine flu vaccine, Donald believes that although the virus can be deadly, it is very unlikely that it will be. The author concludes that, for her, not vaccinating was the right decision, and she urges others to make their own informed decision. Donald is an elementary school teacher in Waterloo, Ontario, in Canada.

AS YOU READ, CONSIDER THE FOLLOWING QUESTIONS:
1. The author suggests that the Canadian government's urging of citizens to get vaccinated may be driven by what motive?
2. Donald claims that her son's risk of getting swine flu is outweighed by his risk of what happening?
3. Donald has chosen to take what precaution against swine flu instead of a vaccine?

H1N1—to take it or not to take it—that is the question. I wonder what Macbeth would have done. I definitely have my opinions on vaccinations; however, I have always felt that it is a very personal decision that should be made by an informed person. Because this vaccination has played out like no other, it has become increasingly difficult to make an informed decision. Being faced with an expectation of a pandemic similar to the one that hit Mexico last spring, seeing body bags being delivered to native reserves, hearing the constant barrage of news releases from health officials urging everyone to roll up their sleeves, and experiencing hour-long lineups has resulted in a frenzy of panic and fear.

People gather at an H1N1 information table in California. According to the author, people trying to make an informed decision about being vaccinated are confronted with a public fearful of an H1N1 pandemic and an endless stream of press releases from health officials.

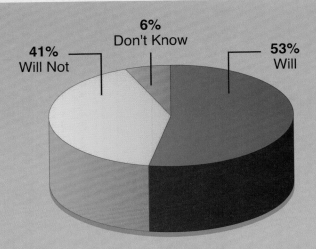

Public Opinion on Swine Flu Vaccination, September 2009

Do you think you, personally, will or will not get this vaccine?

6%
Don't Know

41%
Will Not

53%
Will

Taken from: Harvard Opinion Research Program, "Public Views of the H1N1 Vaccine," September 14–20, 2009.

To Vaccinate or Not

While we wait for our fix, let's take time to process the other information that comes our way. According to Health Canada (as reported on Canada AM) the H1N1 strain that is presently passing through our community is milder than originally anticipated. It makes me wonder how much serum our government purchased and what expiry date it contains. It would certainly explain the further government expense of two-sided, glossy flyers which have recently been sent to homeowners urging them to get their shots. With the tight economy and my ever-increasing taxes, I can only wonder about the number of dollars that have been spent on this aggressive campaign.

But, my penny pinching urges give way to my heart as I hear about the many deaths that have occurred due to this virus. Although I am not to worry too much (being old), my son is in the at-risk group. This sends me on another quest for information. As posted on the Public Health Agency [section of] Canada's website, as of Nov. 5th

[2009,] 115 people have died from H1N1 in this country [Canada]. Furthermore, Wikipedia confirms that the population of Canada, as of Nov. 9th, is 33,838,000 people. You do the math (1 in 294,243). Ironically, my son may have a higher chance of getting a serious side effect from the shot (approximately 1 in 100,000), than from dying as a result of the H1N1 virus.

A Decision to Forego Vaccination

As a person who must weigh all sides before jumping head first into something, I still have a lot of questions. And unlike many trusting souls, I cannot take the word of someone just because they have the reputation to "know best." I believe that everyone is capable of knowing what is best for them by taking control of their health through knowledge, healthy eating and exercise.

Dr. [Mehmet] Oz, a famous American surgeon, introduced me to the virus-fighting neti pot. Once a day I rinse my sinuses with luke-warm salt water (using the neti pot) and then I gargle. According to Dr. Oz, a virus (including H1N1) cannot live in a salt water environment and the only way a virus can enter your body is through the nose or mouth. I have used this protocol during the past month, when 15 out of my 26 students were experiencing flu symptoms. I have yet to get sick, or get the flu shot.

For me, for now, I'll stick with my salty nose rinse. It works. It's cheap. There are no side effects and I know what is in it. After much coaxing and seeing how healthy I continue to be, my husband has finally started using the rinse. However, my son is still weighing his options. At the end of the day, after all the conversation, it still comes down to a very personal decision. Make it an informed one.

**EVALUATING THE AUTHORS'
ARGUMENTS:**

In this viewpoint Leslie Donald contends that whether to vaccinate is a personal decision. Give two examples from authors of other viewpoints in this chapter who would disagree with her and explain why.

Viewpoint
6

Refusing to Get the H1N1 Vaccine Is Selfish

Juliet Guichon and Ian Mitchell

"Canadians should consider not just the risks to themselves, their loved ones and those with whom they come into contact, but also to our health-care system."

In the following viewpoint Juliet Guichon and Ian Mitchell argue that people have a duty to get vaccinated against the H1N1, or swine flu, virus. The authors contend that Canadians who do not get vaccinated receive benefits from the public health care system without doing their part to support it. Furthermore, they argue that individual choice to forego vaccination could cause the health care system to collapse, harming many people. Guichon and Mitchell encourage people to remind each other of their responsibility to get vaccinated for the good of all. Guichon holds a doctorate in law and is a senior associate in the Office of Medical Bioethics at the University of Calgary. Mitchell is a professor of pediatrics and bioethics at the University of Calgary.

1. The authors estimate that what percentage of the population will get the swine flu if they are not vaccinated?
2. Guichon and Mitchell claim that people who refuse vaccines are really acting from what?
3. The authors charge that the influenza pandemic requires people to assess personal interest, reconciling it with what duty?

A recent poll indicated that 48 percent of Canadians might refuse the H1N1 vaccination—and that number went up to 51 per cent in an online poll reported in yesterday's *Globe and Mail*. These figures suggest that many Canadians are not considering the public good and have a misguided understanding of their personal interest.

According to Canada's Chief Public Health Officer, David Butler-Jones, the risk of experiencing severe side effects after receiving the shot is one in a million, compared with the 20 to 35 percent of the population who will get sick from this pandemic flu without protection. "If every single Canadian is inoculated," he said, "then 30 Canadians could have the potential for a severe side effect, compared to 10 million people sick, 100,000 people in hospital and 10,000 people dead."

In the face of such numbers, Canadians should consider not just the risks to themselves, their loved ones and those with whom they come in contact, but also to our health-care system.

The public nature of Canadian health care creates both individual rights and individual responsibilities. But people can assert rights to a public resource without recognizing a responsibility toward its limited nature. This problem was brilliantly described in 1968 by ecologist Garrett Hardin in the journal *Science* as "the tragedy of the commons." In this hypothetical case, individual actors operate on self-interest and ultimately destroy a shared limited resource—even when such destruction is clearly not to anyone's long-term benefit. Canadians are familiar with this tragedy because it describes the collapse of the Atlantic cod fishery.

Mass H1N1 vaccination refusal similarly might destroy (at least temporarily) our health-care system, with the threatened 100,000 people in hospital. We have a limited number of hospital beds and respirators and a finite number of people who know how best to use them. Every vaccinated person increases the likelihood that health-care professionals will be free to treat other people. What's more, inoculation reduces transmission. If unvaccinated people make health-care workers sick, they cannot look after other patients.

While the tragedy of the commons can shed light on vaccination choice, it cannot explain why an individual would choose to act against his or her self-interest. (The cod fishers who depleted the fish stocks to the detriment of future generations at least enjoyed immediate personal benefit.)

Although vaccine refusers seem motivated to avoid personal risk, they are really acting from misinformation and a one-sided view of risk. Public-health officials have tried to transfer their considerable knowledge to those fearful of vaccination. But they are up against the Internet, which makes plentiful both good and bad information.

> **FAST FACT**
>
> Statistics Canada reported that although Canada overall lost 30 million working hours in November 2009 due to flu illness, 10.5 percent of health care workers reported working more hours.

Moreover, lay people can be confused by publicly available scientific information because they don't understand the scientific method or conversations scientists have among themselves. If a scientist were 99 percent certain that something is true, the scientist would reveal and discuss the 1 percent uncertainty. Therefore, for lay people to state that the scientist is uncertain is to misstate the conversation.

Some vaccination refusers also imply that public-health officials are in the pocket of the pharmaceutical industry. But *we* pay these officials to act in the public interest. And, almost certainly, their moral disposition *is* to act in the public interest. Moreover, the Canadian public service has systems to ensure that its officials are not directed by private or foreign interests.

A Canadian family waits to receive H1N1 vaccinations. Despite the availability of universal health care in the country, almost 50 percent of Canadians refused to be vaccinated.

If half of Canadians refuse vaccination, our limited health-care resources (people, medical supplies and physical infrastructure) will probably be depleted. How can we avoid such a tragedy?

This year's Nobel Prize in economics was awarded to Elinor Ostrom for demonstrating that if those people who are threatened by the depletion of scarce resources repeatedly interact, then they change their behaviour to safeguard the threatened commons.

Such interaction includes talking. Perhaps the gravity of the current situation requires unusually frank conversation among Canadians, such as, "My diabetic child needs ongoing access to health care that you, refusing H1N1 vaccination for yourself and your children, might block."

It seems better to have these conversations now than next year when it might be too awful to speak about how vaccination refusal put such a strain on health-care resources that loved ones with other conditions died.

Canadians share a common plight: an influenza pandemic; an already overstretched public health-care system tending to a vulnerable and aging population; the availability of a safe and effective H1N1 vaccine; and our Chief Public Health Officer's recommendation to become vaccinated as soon as possible.

These facts require citizens to decide how best to assess personal interest and to reconcile it with the duty to protect the public good.

We are entitled to share in limited health-care resources. How much will we demand? We are invited to be vaccinated against H1N1. How will we each respond?

EVALUATING THE AUTHORS' ARGUMENTS:

In this viewpoint Juliet Guichon and Ian Mitchell rely on the fact that Canada's health care system is a public good in concluding that Canadians have a responsibility to uphold it. Does the fact that the United States lacks such a health care system mean that their argument does not work in America? Explain your answer.

Chapter 3

How Can Vaccines Be Improved?

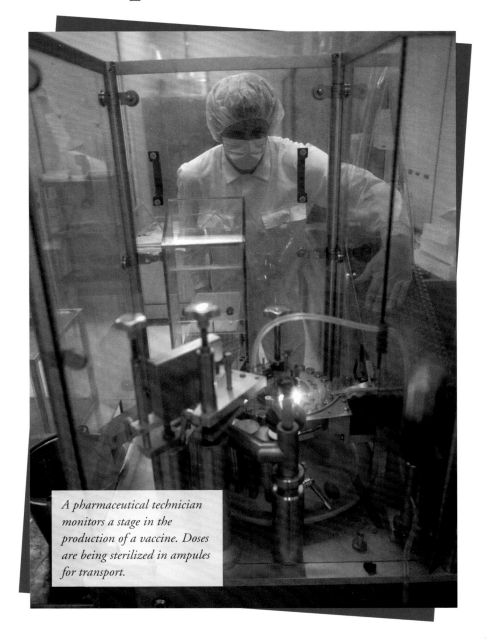

A pharmaceutical technician monitors a stage in the production of a vaccine. Doses are being sterilized in ampules for transport.

New Technology Is Needed to Eliminate Flu Vaccine Shortages

Henry I. Miller

"Developing these new technologies for mass production is essential if we want to be prepared for the next pandemic."

In the following viewpoint Henry I. Miller argues that the current vaccine production system is outdated and that new technologies are needed to produce flu vaccines more quickly. He contends that the vaccine shortages that occurred in the United States during the 2009 H1N1 flu season should serve as a wake-up call for health officials to address this issue. Moreover, he says, if the 2009 H1N1 virus had been more deadly, these vaccine shortages could have led to social unrest. Miller suggests two new technologies—DNA technology and cell-based technology—as promising for future flu vaccines. Miller is a physician and fellow at Stanford University's Hoover Institution. He is the author of *To America's Health: A Proposal to Reform the FDA.*

AS YOU READ, CONSIDER THE FOLLOWING QUESTIONS:
1. According to the author, how old is the current vaccine production system?
2. Miller claims that DNA technology can be used to create vaccines in what length of time after the viral DNA is isolated?
3. In June 2009 the US Department of Health and Human Services awarded a contract of what value to Protein Sciences for developing gene-based technology for vaccines?

The H1N1 swine flu has sickened at least 22 million and killed almost 4,000 in the United States since April [2009 to December 2009] according to the Centers for Disease Control and Prevention.

The shortage of the promised supplies of H1Nl flu vaccine has led to long waits in clinic lines for many Americans, frantic calls to doctors' offices, and growing concern that immunization will arrive too late to prevent illness. In high-risk populations such as asthmatics, young children and expectant mothers, that anxiety is fueled by the possibility of life-threatening consequences should they become infected.

H1N1 Provides a Wake-Up Call

Overall, though, we were lucky this time around. Vaccine manufacturers have been able to produce substantial amounts of vaccine in record time and, as flu viruses go, the current H1N1 is tame. But the H1N1 immunization effort should be a wake-up call to health officials: We are woefully unprepared to deal with a true pandemic of a highly lethal virus. We need to modernize the technology used to make vaccines, so that they can be developed and manufactured more quickly. If large numbers of people were being killed by H1N1, shortages of vaccine would cause riots.

The trouble with our current vaccine production system is that it is not rapidly scalable to demand. It is an 80-year-old system that depends on harvesting the vaccine from fertilized chicken eggs. Manufacturers grow the virus in the eggs until there is a sufficiently high titer [concentration of antibodies], and then the virus is harvested, killed and purified.

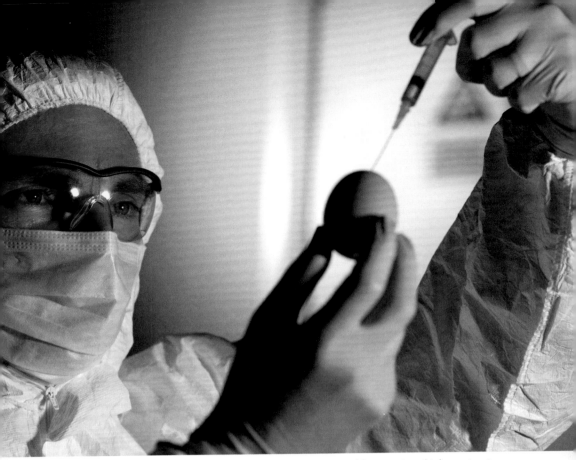

Current flu vaccine production depends on an eighty-year-old system in which vaccine is harvested from fertilized chicken eggs.

The entire process takes months. To harvest a suitable amount of vaccine for flu season requires millions of eggs. In 21st century America, we are waging war on a lethal infectious disease with World War I–era technology.

New Technology Exists

Fortunately, there are two newer, far superior ways to create vaccines.

The first is a process using recombinant DNA, or "gene-splicing," technology to create a vaccine that induces the body to make its own antigen, and then to produce antibodies to that antigen. Researchers produce DNA of the target virus gene in a laboratory and introduce it into a circle of DNA called a plasmid, which acts as a carrier.

The plasmids containing the viral gene can easily and quickly be grown in large amounts. When the plasmids are injected into the muscle of a subject, they are taken up by cells that use the viral gene to make a viral protein, usually a protein that appears on the surface of the virus. (Sometimes, a second gene is present that directs the synthesis of an internal protein of the flu virus.) The viral protein—which is noninfectious and harmless—enters the bloodstream, where the immune system recognizes it as foreign and starts to make antibodies against it.

If the subject is later exposed to the flu virus, more antibodies are produced and bind to and neutralize the virus. Thus, the plasmid DNA that contains the viral gene is the vaccine.

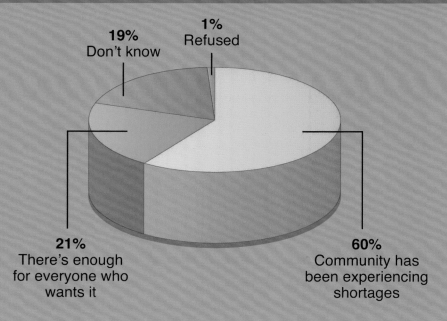

Public Views of H1N1 Vaccine Shortage, November 2009

To the best of your knowledge, is there enough H1N1 flu vaccine in your community right now for everyone who wants to be vaccinated, or has your community been experiencing shortages?

19%
Don't know

1%
Refused

21%
There's enough for everyone who wants it

60%
Community has been experiencing shortages

*Date asked: November 1, 2009

Taken from: Harvard Opinion Research Program, "Public Views of the H1N1 Vaccine Shortage," October 30–November 1, 2009. www.hsph.harvard.edu.

The entire process, once the viral DNA is isolated, takes only a few days. This process is cost-effective and produces a vaccine with numerous advantages over the traditional versions.

DNA vaccines have a high heat tolerance, which means they can be transported over long distances without becoming inactivated, and can be stored in locations (such as developing countries) that lack refrigeration.

The vaccines are also easily altered in the lab, so that if the virus were to mutate, the genetic code could be changed accordingly and production could resume quickly. Another advantage is that because DNA vaccines do not contain whole viruses, there is no threat of viral infection from an immunization.

Another promising new vaccine process uses cell cultures of various kinds as a stand-in for the eggs in the traditional model. Manufacturers expose animal or insect cells grown in tissue culture to live virus, allow it to multiply and then harvest, inactivate and purify the virus particles.

This method saves time in scaling up to meet vaccine needs and avoids relying on eggs, which is cumbersome and could be vulnerable to infection if there were an outbreak of avian flu—thereby creating unacceptable and possibly lethal delays for the production process.

Federal health officials have already recognized the importance of these two cutting-edge approaches. A recent example is a contract from the U.S. Department of Health and Human Services (HHS) to the drug company Novartis, to support a new vaccine manufacturing facility that utilizes cell-based technology and other new processes to produce vaccine. And in June [2009], HHS awarded a $35 million contract to Protein Sciences to develop and test a vaccine produced from gene-based technology.

A Universal Vaccine Is Needed

These investments—and others like them—are good first steps, but we need to go further. Research and testing of DNA vaccines in particular must be expanded. Other vaccine manufacturers should be encouraged to branch into new technologies. The government should provide support for basic and proof-of-principle research. Even in the short term, expanding the use of gene and cell-based vaccine technologies could lead to a flu season without the threat of vaccine shortages.

Eventually, it might even yield the holy grail of flu vaccines—a "universal" vaccine based on the virus' internal proteins, so that it is active on many different strains, year after year. Developing these new technologies for mass production is essential if we want to be prepared for the next pandemic.

EVALUATING THE AUTHOR'S ARGUMENTS:

In this viewpoint Henry I. Miller argues that the federal government needs to make investments in new vaccine technology. Give one reason that could explain why vaccine manufacturers have not made investments in such new technology themselves.

A Vaccine for All Flu Viruses Is Needed to Avoid a Flu Pandemic

John M. Barry

"In the long term, we need a vaccine that works against all influenza viruses."

In the following viewpoint John M. Barry argues that a flu vaccine is needed that will vaccinate people against all strains of influenza, including the recent swine flu and bird flu strains. Barry points out that influenza pandemics are unpredictable and can quickly kill thousands of people. He contends that nonpharmaceutical interventions do only so much to minimize the impact of flu epidemics, so what is really needed is a highly effective vaccine. Barry is Distinguished Scholar at the Center for Bioenvironmental Research of Tulane and Xavier Universities and the author of *The Great Influenza: The Epic Story of the Deadliest Plague in History.*

Last month [June 2009], the World Health Organization finally declared that the new H1N1 virus has become pandemic. Monday [June 29] it reported a big jump in cases and fatalities since last week.

How many people this virus will sicken and kill depends, ultimately, on three things: the virus itself; the impact of what are known as "non-pharmaceutical interventions," or NPIs; and the availability and effectiveness of a vaccine.

Flu Pandemics

The virus will be the most important factor. Influenza is one of the fastest-mutating organisms in existence, which makes it unpredictable, and a virus newly infecting the human population is likely to be even more unpredictable as it adapts to a new environment.

There have been four pandemics that we know about in some detail: 1889–92, 1918–20, 1957–60, and 1968–70.

All four followed similar patterns: initial sporadic activity with local instances of high attack rates—just as H1N1 has behaved so far—followed four to eight months later by waves of widespread illness with 20 percent to 40 percent of the population sickened. (In a normal influenza season about 10 percent of the population gets sick.) Subsequent waves followed as well.

In all four pandemics, lethality changed from wave to wave—sometimes increasing, sometimes decreasing.

It's impossible to know what will happen this time, but in 1999 the Centers for Disease Control and Prevention modeled a moderate pandemic in the United States, including a vaccine in its calculations, and concluded that the death toll would probably be 89,000 to 207,000.

If the virulence of this virus does not significantly increase—and right now there is no reason to think it will—something close to the lower number looks probable.

What could help bring about such a best case? Again, the virus is the most important factor, and we have no control over it.

Interventions for a Pandemic

But we do have non-pharmaceutical interventions and the possibility of a vaccine. Such interventions would come into play primarily in a moderate or severe pandemic.

For a mild one, we may not need to take steps beyond washing hands, exercising "cough etiquette" and keeping the sick at home.

But if the virus increases its virulence, other measures, such as closing schools, urging people to telecommute and even banning public meetings, could mitigate the impact.

However, the usefulness of non-pharmaceutical interventions is limited, and even if they work, their chief impact will be to flatten the pandemic's peak and stretch out the duration of a wave of illness to make it easier to handle.

Consider: Those telecommuting are likely to run into Internet capacity problems, while the impact of closing schools—aside from the burden that creates on working parents and their employers, or on children who get good meals only at school—depends on how much kids congregate while out of school.

And sustaining compliance will be both important and difficult. Scholars Bradley Condon and Tapen Sinha found that in Mexico City this spring [2009], when the government advised wearing masks on public transportation, compliance peaked at 65 percent three days later—but declined to 26 percent only five days after that. This decline came even as the government was taking the extreme measure of closing all nonessential services and businesses. Such behavior does not portend well for sustained compliance with any measure.

The Importance of a Vaccine

The most important human intervention is, of course, a vaccine. There are many unknowns: Because influenza mutates so rapidly, a new vaccine has to be made each year just for seasonal flu.

Vaccines for most diseases approach 100 percent effectiveness, but a good flu vaccine is 70 percent effective; a great one is 90 percent effective. The vaccine in the 2007–08 flu season was only 44 percent effective. Hitting the "good" mark for a new virus that may be changing even more rapidly than seasonal flu will be difficult.

Some students in Mexico wear masks in class as a preventive against swine flu infection. Though the government recommended wearing masks in public, only about 65 percent of the public complied—and this figure dropped to 26 percent within days.

"At last—the new flu vaccine. Hold everything. We've just discovered a newer flu virus," cartoon by S. Harris and www.CartoonStock.com. Copyright © S. Harris. Reproduction rights obtainable from www.CartoonStock.com.

Supply is another problem. In a best case, enough vaccine for the entire U.S. population could be available by October [2009] as long as an adjuvant is used to simultaneously stimulate the immune system, which lessens the need for antigen from the virus itself.

However, if the virus used to make vaccine grows slowly, or if a dose requires more antigen than seasonal flu, or if two doses are required to provide protection, producing that much vaccine could easily stretch deep into 2010. In addition, only about 30 percent of the supply will be made in the United States. The more virulent the virus, the more likely it is that foreign governments will refuse to allow export of the vaccine until their own populations are fully protected.

Meanwhile, the emergence of the H1N1 virus in no way lessens the threat from H5N1, more commonly known as bird flu. Shortly before the World Health Organization declared H1N1 a pandemic on June 11, 2009, Egypt confirmed its 78th human case of H5N1, of which 27 had been fatal.

The bottom line? Little can be done in the short term beyond exerting diplomatic pressure to guarantee that foreign governments allow manufacturers to honor contracts to export vaccine.

In the medium term, sustained investment in vaccine production technologies—especially recombinant ones—could make it possible to produce massive amounts of vaccine in a few weeks.

In the long term, we need a vaccine that works against all influenza viruses. Enough work has been done to suggest that this Holy Grail is achievable.

Had influenza been taken seriously for the past 30 years, we would probably have one by now. No matter what happens over the next year or two, that's one history lesson we need to learn.

EVALUATING THE AUTHOR'S ARGUMENTS:

In this viewpoint John M. Barry suggests developing a flu vaccine that would work against all flu viruses. Assuming a vaccine that was 100 percent effective were developed, what would need to happen in order for people never to get the flu?

Mass Vaccination Efforts Are Problematic

Vivienne Parry

In the following viewpoint Vivienne Parry argues that vaccination is not always the solution in preparing for a flu pandemic. She claims that it is difficult for manufacturers to create an effective vaccine in the right quantities for any particular flu virus. Parry contends that one of the dangers of relying on vaccines to deal with a pandemic is the danger of overreacting. She cites the serious problems caused by a mass vaccination program in the United States in 1976 as an example supporting the view that mass vaccination is not always the answer and that such programs may do more harm than good. Parry is a science journalist and the author of *The Truth About Hormones*.

"Vaccination has to be carefully considered."

1. According to the author, what flu sub-type do many assume will cause the next pandemic?
2. The author discusses a mass vaccination program set off in 1976 by the death of a soldier who died from a variant of what flu virus?
3. Parry claims that how many people developed Guillain-Barré Syndrome as a side effect from the vaccines of 1976?

The first question on people's lips when the spectre of pandemic flu looms large is often: "Is there a vaccine and where can I get it?" That question is no doubt being asked again now [April 2009] with the outbreak of swine flu in Mexico.

Preparing for a Flu Pandemic

Flu is an awesome foe because it is so slippery, constantly changing its colours. Every year the World Health Organisation decides which strains are likely to be most prevalent in the following year and bases the annual flu vaccinations on this combination.

Many assume that H5N1 [bird flu] will be the pandemic flu sub-type and that it will emerge from the Far East. Indeed, some pharmaceutical manufacturers are banking on it. GlaxoSmithKline [GSK], for instance, it has committed $2 billion to conduct research and expand capacity for its its antiviral drug Relenza, along with a new H5N1 vaccine, which was given marketing authorisation in all 27 EU [European Union] member states a year ago. But the truth is that pandemic flu could arise from another strain altogether, from an entirely different quarter of the world. Like Mexico for instance.

The GSK product and a number of those from other manufacturers are generic, not specific H5N1 vaccines. They do not offer full immunity but are likely to reduce symptoms and deaths. The UK [United Kingdom] is currently stockpiling 3.3 million doses, which, in the event of an outbreak, are likely to be given first to frontline healthcare workers.

To produce a vaccine for a specific pandemic the exact strain has to be isolated and "tamed" so that it is safe for manufacture. From isolation to first shot in an arm takes at least 20 weeks—just for the first batches. By the time there is enough for the entire British population the outbreak could be over. Hence Britain's strategy to stockpile the generic vaccine in addition to putting plans in place for specific ones.

Biological manufacture is not like manufacturing cars. Flu vaccines are difficult to produce. Most are grown in eggs—one vaccine shot, one egg. It requires huge flocks of birds. If manufacturers focus on specific strains there is no capacity for regular flu treatments, which means that in the UK up to 25,000 more winter deaths would occur.

The Dangers of Overreacting

The dangers of overreacting to a flu pandemic are well known to the Centres for Disease Control [CDC] in Atlanta. In January 1976 an 18-year-old American army recruit, Private David Lewis, collapsed after an all-night training exercise. He died a few hours later in the base hospital of Fort Dix, New Jersey. Like about 300 other recruits he had complained of typical flu symptoms but Private Lewis had ignored the medical officer's orders to go to bed and went off on his exercise.

His death was caused by a previously unknown variant of swine flu A/H1N1. What really spooked the CDC was its similarity to the strain that killed more than 40 million people worldwide in 1918.

The CDC rightly decided to develop a swine flu vaccine for use in the following flu season. Despite careful planning, the national influenza vaccination programme went wrong from the outset. Two doses of vaccine were expected from each egg used, but only one materialised, setting back the timetable dramatically. Then doctors discovered that the vaccine doses that worked well for adults did not protect children effectively. At this point there were only four million doses for 57 million children.

Just as the programme seemed dead on its feet an outbreak of fatal pneumonia broke out at the Pennsylvania Convention of the American Legion, killing 29 people. This was later identified as Legionnaire's disease, hence its name. The media linked it with swine flu and politicians joined in the clamour to push forward the swine flu vaccination programme.

Tens of thousands of eggs were required to develop one jar of concentrated vaccine in 1976. Four major flu vaccine manufacturers produced the vaccine in an effort to mass immunize Americans.

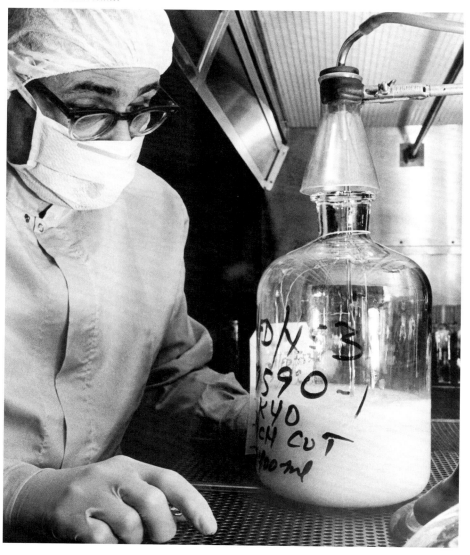

American Perception of Government Handling of the Swine Flu Pandemic, Novemer 2009

Is the federal government doing a good job, a poor job, or neither a good nor a poor job of handling the swine flu pandemic?

Total good	47
Very good job	14
Somewhat good job	33
Neither a good nor a poor job	22
Total poor	29
Somewhat poor job	15
Very poor job	14
Don't know	2

Taken from: AP-GFK Poll, November 5–November 9, 2009. http://surveys.ap.org.

Mass Vaccination

The threat from swine flu was vastly exaggerated, so that eventually the President, Gerald Ford, took charge. A mass vaccination went ahead even after it became clear that swine flu was not a danger. In fact, Private Lewis was the only person to die from a mere 300 cases. The programme cost more than $200 million and as a side-effect there were thousands more regular flu deaths because of a lack of vaccine.

Another rare and fatal side-effect occured in about nine in every million of those vaccinated, who developed Guillain Barré Syndrome [GBS], a paralytic disease. When so many are involved, rarities become numerous. There were 500 cases and 25 deaths from GBS. The vaccination programme was stopped, having only treated 24 per cent of the population. And because the US Government had indemnified the vaccine manufacturers before the programme began (because American insurers wouldn't take on the risk) they had to pay out an additional £39 million in compensation claims.

The point is not that mass vaccination is wrong. Far from it. But vaccination has to be carefully considered. The risks have to be clearly balanced against the benefits, decisions have to be taken on the science not the politics and frequently re-evaluated. For the one thing that will never change is flu's capacity to surprise us.

EVALUATING THE AUTHORS' ARGUMENTS:

In this viewpoint Vivienne Parry cautions against assuming that vaccination is always the solution when dealing with a flu pandemic. Do you think the two previous authors in this chapter would agree with her on this point? Why or why not?

Viewpoint

4

More Time and Money Should Be Invested in Developing an AIDS Vaccine

"No public health intervention is more powerful or cost-effective against infectious disease than a vaccine."

Seth Berkley

In the following viewpoint Seth Berkley argues that pessimism about the possibility of developing an AIDS vaccine is unwarranted. He points to a recent study in Thailand as evidence that progress is being made in the development of such a vaccine. Berkley cautions that even if the recent study is not ultimately fruitful, an AIDS vaccine is still the best solution to the global AIDS crisis, and scientists should continue to work on its development. Berkley is a medical doctor and the president of the International AIDS Vaccine Initiative, a nonprofit organization working to ensure the development of preventive HIV vaccines for use throughout the world.

AS YOU READ, CONSIDER THE FOLLOWING QUESTIONS:

1. The author claims that private and public spending on development of an AIDS vaccine declined by what percentage between 2007 and 2008?
2. Berkley says that on the first analysis of a study in Thailand, a vaccine combination was shown to reduce the risk of HIV infection by what percentage?
3. How many new HIV infections occur daily, according to the author?

Vaccine researchers don't often find themselves at the center of public controversies. But a storm has erupted over the announcement last month [September 2009] that an experimental AIDS vaccine tested in Thailand proved modestly effective. It was billed as a major scientific advance—the long-awaited hard evidence that it is possible to inoculate people against AIDS. But now the trial has been called into question in a way that is overblown and possibly destructive.

Pessimism About an AIDS Vaccine

At a biotech conference last week, I asked a major industry scientist what he thought of the Thai trial announcement, and, although no additional data had been presented, he replied simply, "I don't believe it." Unfortunately, such pessimism may be hard to dispel and may ultimately thwart other efforts to develop an AIDS vaccine.

Even before this controversy erupted, it had been an effort to maintain sufficient support for AIDS vaccine research and development. In 2008, private and public spending on this vital mission declined by 10 percent from the year before. A few fanatical AIDS activists have even called for ending the American government's considerable support for AIDS vaccine research, and spending the money instead on AIDS treatment. Patient care is vital, of course, but it alone can only mitigate, not end, the pandemic.

This is why it is essential to clear things up.

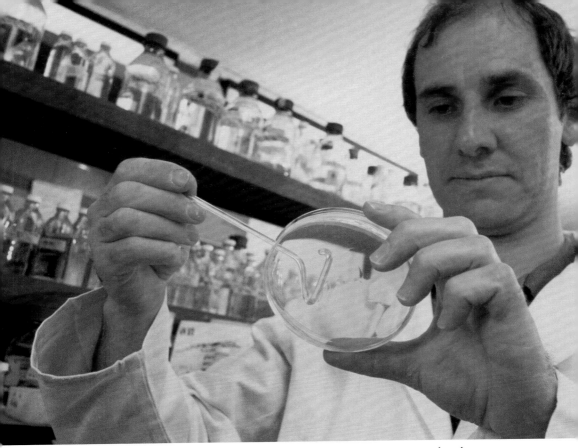

As part of research for an AIDS vaccine, a scientist uses a glass loop to spread and grow recombinant bacteria on agar in a petri dish. It has become increasingly difficult to sustain sufficient support for AIDS research.

A Promising Study in Thailand

The Thai study was the largest AIDS vaccine trial yet, following 16,402 volunteers for six years. It was a collaborative effort by, among others, the United States military, the National Institutes of Health and the Thai Health Ministry. (The organization I head, a nonprofit that conducts vaccine research and development but was not involved and has no commercial interest in the candidates tested.) The trial partners initially announced that the vaccine combination reduced the risk of infection by 31.2 percent in a statistically significant analysis.

A few days later, the trial collaborators began to brief researchers privately about additional data, including a second type of analysis that indicated the vaccine regimen had been slightly less effective than the first analysis suggested. This second analysis was not statistically significant, meaning that chance, rather than the protective effect of the vaccine candidate, might explain why fewer volunteers in the vaccinated group than in the placebo group were infected with H.I.V.

Some researchers questioned why both analyses weren't announced at the same time—which certainly would have been preferable—and suggested to reporters that the second analysis called the first one into doubt. The trial sponsors say they thought the complexities of the second analysis and all additional data were best explored in a peer-reviewed paper in a scientific journal and at a presentation at the AIDS Vaccine Conference in Paris this week [in October 2009]. But with news outlets reporting that the trial results may be a fluke, there is a risk that they will be forever tainted, whatever the final analyses show. What's more, the stain of dubiousness may remain on all AIDS vaccine research and development.

The Need for an AIDS Vaccine

That would be a shame. Although the candidate duo tested in the Thai trial did not prove to be a vaccine ready for the market, it may provide an unprecedented opportunity to learn how an AIDS vaccine can work. A comparison of blood samples from volunteers could indicate what specific immune responses the combination may have activated to provide protection. If so, this knowledge could help scientists improve upon the more promising candidates that have emerged since the trial candidates were designed a decade ago, and determine which ones are most likely to work.

This illustrates why the controversy over statistical significance is exaggerated. Whether you consider the first or second analysis, the observed effect of the Thai candidates was either just above or below the level of statistical significance. Statisticians will tell you it is possible to observe an effect and have

> **FAST FACT**
>
> According to the International AIDS Vaccine Initiative, more than 25 million people worldwide have died from AIDS, 33 million people are living with HIV, and nearly 3 million become newly infected each year.

The Potential Impact of an AIDS Vaccine

Vaccine scenarios	Vaccine efficacy	Percentage of population given vaccine	New infections averted, 2015–1030	Percentage of new infections averted	Projected Annual HIV infections in 2030
LOW	30%	20%	2.1 million	9%	1.3 million
MEDIUM	50%	30%	5.6 million	24%	1.0 million
HIGH	70%	40%	9.8 million	41%	600,000
VERY HIGH	90%	40%	12.0 million	50%	500,000

Taken from: International AIDS Vaccine Initiative (IAVI), "Estimating the Potential Impact of an AIDS Vaccine in Developing Countries," IAVI Policy Note, August 20, 2009.

reason to think it's real even if it's not statistically significant. And if you think it's real, you ought to examine it carefully.

Even if the Thai vaccine regimen turns out, on examination, to have had no real benefit, researchers will still learn from the trial, as they do from every study. Moreover, other noteworthy advances featured at the Paris conference this week will offer fresh hope for an AIDS vaccine. Years of investment and dogged science are providing leads for solving one of today's most pressing research challenges. Some 7,400 new H.I.V. infections occur daily throughout the world. Clearly we need better methods of preventing the spread of H.I.V., and no public health intervention is more powerful or cost-effective against infectious disease than a vaccine.

EVALUATING THE AUTHOR'S ARGUMENTS:

In this viewpoint Seth Berkley says that an AIDS vaccine is the best way to curb the spread of HIV. If true, does this mean that unlimited amounts of time and money should be spent on research to develop a vaccine? Why or why not?

No More Research Money Should Be Spent on an AIDS Vaccine

Homayoon Khanlou and Michael Weinstein

"It is time to pull the plug on US public funding for HIV vaccine research."

In the following viewpoint Homayoon Khanlou and Michael Weinstein argue that it is a mistake to continue to pour money and research time into the development of an AIDS vaccine. The authors claim that over twenty-five years of research have yielded no promising results and that the money currently spent on vaccine research would have more effective results if spent elsewhere. Khanlou and Weinstein claim that scientists have come to a consensus that it is unlikely that there will ever be an AIDS vaccine and conclude that the United States should respond by halting research funding. Khanlou is chief of medicine, United States, at the AIDS Healthcare Foundation (AHF) and Weinstein is president of the AHF, a global organization providing HIV/AIDS medicine and advocacy to over one hundred thousand people in twenty-two countries.

Homayoon Khanlou and Michael Weinstein, "No Results? No Research Money," *Los Angeles Times*, April 25, 2008. Copyright © 2008 by Homayoon Khanlou and Michael Weinstein. Reproduced by permission.

The search for an AIDS vaccine has lost its scientific purpose and turned into a self-serving quest.

AIDS Vaccine Research

How else to explain the remarks found in David Baltimore and Seth Berkley's "Keep funding the AIDS vaccine"? Saying simply that "AIDS vaccine development is hard" is not a credible response to recent criticism leveled at the ballooning U.S. budget for AIDS vaccine research and the meager results it has produced. The argument is particularly weak when you consider that nearly $1 billion in public funding is poured annually into this fruitless quest, while millions globally lack access to the revolutionary, life-saving AIDS treatment that was developed more than 12 years ago: antiretroviral medication.

The recent Merck vaccine trial that Baltimore and Berkley mention was not only a failure, it actually endangered lives by increasing the likelihood that study participants would contract the virus. The Merck trial was also not an anomaly. There have been 25 years of repeated AIDS vaccine failures at high cost to taxpayers. To call for more human clinical research—as Baltimore and Berkley do—defies common sense and endangers lives. Important insights into the basic mechanisms of the virus and the human body's response to it are still missing. So where is the science to back up their call for more money? And can such an expense be justified if measured in human lives lost because of lack of access to treatment that can cost as little as 50 cents a day?

The Best Approach to HIV/AIDS

The best way to break the chain of infection is to prevent an infected person from passing it on to others. A number of extraordinarily effective approaches to achieve this already exist. The spread of infection would be significantly curbed if we focused primarily on the source of all new infections: the 33 million people who are currently estimated to be carrying the virus. Effective pre- and/or post-exposure prophylaxis [prevention] treatments are an example of a possible approach. A

A technician draws blood as part of Merck Pharmaceutical's AIDs vaccine trial in which 16,402 volunteers were immunized. The author says the trial was a failure, not only because it was expensive but because it also put the trial subjects' lives at risk.

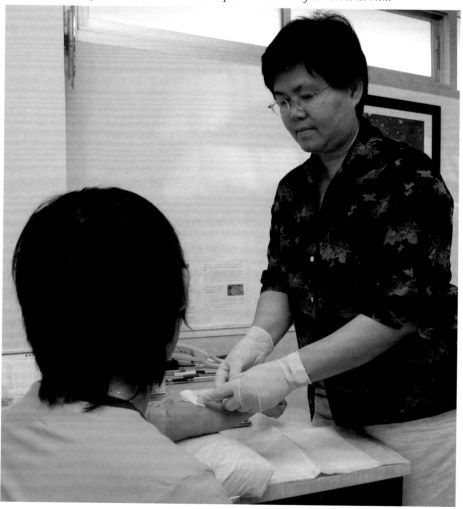

focused antiretroviral pre-prophylaxis effort in high-risk populations, such as commercial sex workers, would be a highly cost-effective way to prevent the spread of infection.

There is also mounting evidence to demonstrate that patients with undetectable viral loads—achieved through antiretroviral treatment—have a much lower rate of transmission, perhaps a rate even lower than could be achieved with a successful vaccine. Still, these lifesaving drugs are currently unavailable to all but the smallest fraction of the people who need them. What might a nearly $1-billion annual investment in the worldwide scale-up of antiretroviral treatment buy in terms of transmissions prevented?

Consensus Among Scientists

In a post–Merck-failure research climate, the scientific community has come to a consensus: an investment in basic science is needed. Such research does not require the enormous, and enormously expensive, global clinical trial apparatus currently in place for AIDS vaccine research. In fact, according to recent reports, researchers with Berkley's International AIDS Vaccine Initiative and the Center for HIV/ AIDS Vaccine Immunology— employing funds from the U.S. HIV vaccine research pot—plan to focus on such areas of basic science research as the genetic sequencing of new HIV viruses, an investigation into how genetic factors might control HIV infection and inquiry into the possible reasons why some people exposed to HIV do not progress to AIDS. However, the U.S. government already allocates several billion dollars a year to funding basic AIDS research. So what is the purpose of setting aside another $1 billion annually under a separate HIV vaccine research umbrella?

FAST FACT

According to AVERT, an international AIDS charity, only 42 percent of people needing AIDS treatment in developing and transitional countries were receiving it at the end of 2008.

To date, there has been no evidence that there will ever be an AIDS vaccine. In fact, in a poll of more than 35 top HIV/AIDS scientists in

The Views of Leading AIDS Researchers on an AIDS Vaccine, 2008

Are you more or less optimistic about the prospects of an HIV vaccine compared to a year ago?

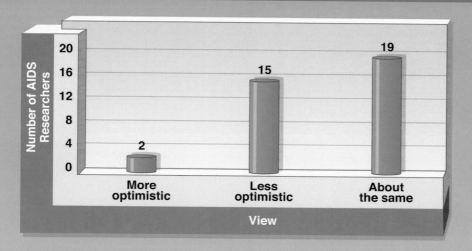

Do you agree that we now need to change the direction of HIV vaccine research given the failure of clinical trials so far?

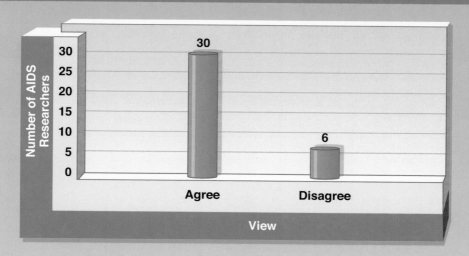

Britain and the U.S. conducted by Britain's *Independent* newspaper and published this week [April 24, 2008], "nearly two-thirds believed that an HIV vaccine will not be developed within the next 10 years" and a "substantial minority of the scientists admitted that an HIV vaccine may never be developed."

Resources are not limitless. To date, there has been no evidence that there will ever be an AIDS vaccine. It is time for an honest reassessment of funding priorities and a redeployment of resources into delivering antiretroviral medications to the people who need it. It is time to pull the plug on U.S. public funding for HIV vaccine research.

After all, can you think of any other U.S. enterprise that has been studied and investigated for 25 years and on which many billions of dollars have been spent without any results?

EVALUATING THE AUTHORS' ARGUMENTS:

In this viewpoint Homayoon Khanlou and Michael Weinstein claim that money spent over the past twenty-five years on research for an AIDS vaccine could have been better spent on antiretroviral treatment that helps save the lives of people already infected with HIV. How do you think that Seth Berkley, author of the previous viewpoint, would respond to the claim that the money would be better spent in this way? Explain how Berkley might defend his position.

Facts About Vaccines

Editor's note: These facts can be used in reports to add credibility when making important points or claims.

US Government Recommendations on Vaccines

The Centers for Disease Control and Prevention recommends childhood vaccination against the following diseases (multiple doses are usually necessary for immunization):

- Diphtheria, tetanus, pertussis (DTaP or TDaP) vaccine: Diphtheria is a bacterial respiratory disease that is transmitted by coughing and sneezing and can result in death if untreated. Tetanus, or lockjaw, is a bacterial disease of the nervous system that enters the body through a break in the skin and kills about 10 to 20 percent of those who get it. Pertussis, or whooping cough, is a highly contagious respiratory disease caused by bacteria, which can result in death, especially in infants.

- Hepatitis A vaccine: Hepatitis A is a viral disease that damages the liver and is usually spread through the ingestion of stool infected with the virus.

- Hepatitis B vaccine: Hepatitis B is a viral disease that attacks the liver, which can cause lifelong infection, liver failure, and death. Spread through blood, semen, or other body fluid, Hepatitis B can be transmitted during birth, sex, and contact with infected blood.

- Hib (*Haemophilus influenzae* type b) vaccine: Hib is a type of bacteria that can cause meningitis, pneumonia, epiglottitis, and other infections that can be life threatening or cause permanent damage.

- Human papillomavirus, or HPV, vaccine (females only): HPV is a virus spread through sexual contact and can result in cervical cancer.

- Influenza vaccine (yearly): Influenza, or flu, is a contagious viral disease that causes mild to serious illness, occasionally resulting in death. The specific type of virus and severity of the disease can vary widely, and different vaccines are needed for different strains of the flu.

- Measles, mumps, rubella (MMR) vaccine: Measles is a highly contagious viral disease that still kills about 200,000 people each year around the world. Mumps is a contagious viral disease that is rare in the United States. Rubella, or German measles, is an acute viral disease that can result in organ damage and, for pregnant woman who acquire it, birth defects.
- Meningococcal vaccine: Meningococcal disease, or meningitis, can be a viral or bacterial infection, with the latter sometimes causing permanent brain damage and hearing loss.
- Pneumococcal vaccine: Pneumococcal disease, such as pneumococcal pneumonia, bacteremia, meningitis, and otitis media are bacterial diseases caused by pneumococcus that can result in long-term health problems and death.
- Poliovirus vaccine: Poliomyelitis, or polio, is a highly infectious viral disease that attacks the nervous system, sometimes resulting in permanent disability or death.
- Rotavirus vaccine: Rotavirus is a viral gastrointestinal disease that causes vomiting and diarrhea and and results in over 500,000 deaths in children each year around the globe.
- Varicella vaccine: Varicella, or chicken pox, is a contagious viral infection of the skin that can lead to swelling of the brain and pneumonia.

State Mandatory Vaccine Requirements

- All fifty states have mandatory vaccination laws for public school attendance.
- All fifty states allow for medical exemptions to mandatory school vaccination laws.
- All states except for Mississippi and West Virginia allow religious exemptions to mandatory school vaccination laws.
- Nineteen states—Arizona, Arkansas, California, Colorado, Idaho, Louisiana, Maine, Michigan, Minnesota, New Mexico, North Dakota, Ohio, Oklahoma, Pennsylvania, Texas, Utah, Vermont, Washington, and Wisconsin—also allow philosophical, or personal belief, exemptions to mandatory school vaccination laws.

US Vaccination Rates

According to the National Immunization Survey (NIS), sponsored by the National Center for Immunizations and Respiratory Diseases (NCIRD) and conducted jointly by NCIRD and the National Center for Health Statistics (NCHS), Centers for Disease Control and Prevention, it is estimated that infants aged nineteen to thirty-five months were vaccinated at the following rates (for the minimum recommended dosage):

- Diphtheria, tetanus, pertussis (DTaP) vaccine: 85 percent had received at least four doses.
- Hepatitis A vaccine: 44 percent had received at least two doses.
- Hepatitis B vaccine: 93 percent had received at least three doses.
- Hib (*Haemophilus influenzae* type b) vaccine: 87 percent had received at least three doses.
- Measles, mumps, rubella (MMR) vaccine: 92 percent had received at least one dose.
- Pneumococcal vaccine: 81 percent had received at least four doses.
- Poliovirus vaccine: 94 percent had received at least three doses.
- Varicella vaccine: 91 percent had received at least one dose.

It is estimated by the NIS that in 2009 adolescents aged 13 to 17 years were vaccinated at the following rates (for the minimum recommended dosage):

- Hepatitis B vaccine: 90 percent had received at least three doses.
- Human papillomavirus, or HPV, vaccine (females only): 27 percent had received at least three doses.
- Measles, mumps, rubella (MMR) vaccine: 89 percent had received at least two doses.
- Meningococcal vaccine: 54 percent had received at least one dose.
- Tetanus, diphtheria, pertussis (TDaP) vaccine: 56 percent had received at least one dose since the age of 10.
- Varicella vaccine: 76 percent had received at least two doses or had a history of the disease (chicken pox).

Organizations to Contact

The editors have compiled the following list of organizations concerned with the issues debated in this book. The descriptions are derived from materials provided by the organizations. All have publications or information available for interested readers. The list was compiled on the date of publication of the present volume; the information provided here may change. Be aware that many organizations take several weeks or longer to respond to inquiries, so allow as much time as possible for the receipt of requested materials.

Association of American Physicians and Surgeons (AAPS)
1601 N. Tucson Blvd., Ste. 9
Tucson, AZ 85716-3450
(800) 635-1196
fax: (520) 325-4230
e-mail: aaps@aapsonline.org
website: www.aapsonline.org

The AAPS is a national association of physicians dedicated to preserving freedom in the one-on-one patient-physician relationship. The AAPS fights in the courts for the rights of patients and physicians, sponsors seminars for physicians, testifies on invitation before committees in Congress, and educates the public. Among the news briefs and publications available at the AAPS website are a fact sheet on mandatory vaccines and the organization's resolution concerning mandatory vaccines.

Centers for Disease Control and Prevention (CDC)
1600 Clifton Rd.
Atlanta, GA 30333
(800) 232-4636
e-mail: cdcinfo@cdc.gov
website: www.cdc.gov

The CDC, a part of the US Department of Health and Human Services, is the primary federal agency for conducting and supporting public health activities in the United States. Through research and education, the CDC is dedicated to protecting health and promoting quality of life through the prevention and control of disease, injury, and disability. Among the many publications available at the CDC's website regarding vaccines and immunizations are childhood, adolescent, and adult immunization schedules; information about reasons to vaccinate and the importance of vaccinating; and vaccine safety reports, including access to the Vaccine Adverse Event Reporting System (VAERS).

The Commonwealth Fund
1 E. Seventy-fifth St.
New York, NY 10021
(212) 606-3800
fax: (212) 606-3500
e-mail: info@cmwf.org
website: www.commonwealthfund.org

The Commonwealth Fund is a private foundation that aims to promote a high-performing health care system that achieves better access, improved quality, and greater efficiency, particularly for society's most vulnerable, including low-income people, the uninsured, minority Americans, young children, and elderly adults. The Commonwealth Fund carries out this mandate by supporting independent research on health care issues and making grants to improve health care practice and policy. The foundation publishes *The Commonwealth Fund Digest* and has performance snapshots, such as that on the issue of immunization of young children, available at its website.

Immunization Action Coalition (IAC)
1573 Selby Ave., Ste. 234
St. Paul, MN 55104
(651) 647-9009
fax: (651) 647-9131
e-mail: admin@immunize.org
website: www.immunize.org

The IAC works to increase immunization rates and prevent disease. The IAC creates educational materials and facilitates communication about the safety, efficacy, and use of vaccines within the broad immunization community of patients, parents, health care organizations, and government health agencies. The IAC publishes numerous brochures and vaccination schedules, including the brochure "What If You Don't Immunize Your Child?"

Institute for Vaccine Safety (IVS)
Johns Hopkins Bloomberg School of Public Health
615 N. Wolfe St., Rm. W5041
Baltimore, MD 21205
(410) 955-2955
fax: (410) 502-6733
e-mail: info@hopkinsvaccine.org
website: www.vaccinesafety.edu

The IVS is an institute at the Johns Hopkins Bloomberg School of Public Health with the goal of obtaining and disseminating objective information on the safety of recommended immunizations. The IVS provides a forum for dissemination of data regarding specific issues concerning the safety of immunizations, investigates safety questions, and conducts research. The IVS sponsors academic publications, provides information about state school vaccination law exemptions, and provides information on vaccine legislation.

National Network for Immunization Information (NNii)
301 University Blvd.
Galveston, TX 77555-0350
(409) 772-0199
fax: (409) 772-5208
e-mail: nnii@i4ph.org
website: www.immunizationinfo.org

The NNii is an affiliation of the Infectious Diseases Society of America, the Pediatric Infectious Diseases Society, the American Academy of Pediatrics, the American Nurses Association, the American Academy of Family Physicians, the National Association of Pediatric Nurse Practitioners, the American College of Obstetricians and Gynecologists, the University of Texas Medical Branch, the Society for Adolescent Medicine, and the American Medical Association. The NNii provides the public, health professionals, policy makers, and the media with up-to-date information related to immunization to help them understand the issues and make informed decisions. The NNii publishes numerous briefs, papers, and pamphlets, including "Do Multiple Vaccines Overwhelm the Immune System?," available at its website.

National Vaccine Information Center (NVIC)
407 Church St., Ste. H
Vienna, VA 22180
(703) 938-0342
fax: (703) 938-5768
e-mail: contactNVIC@gmail.com
web ite: www.nvic.org

The NVIC is dedicated to defending the right to informed consent to medical interventions and to preventing vaccine injuries and deaths through public education. The NVIC provides assistance to those who have suffered vaccine reactions; promotes research to evaluate vaccine safety and effectiveness; and monitors vaccine research, development, regulation, policy making, and legislation. Many resources are available at the NVIC's website, including position papers and articles, among which is "Promoting Vaccination, Fear, Hate & Discrimination."

ThinkTwice Global Vaccine Institute
PO Box 9638
Santa Fe, NM 87504
(505) 983-1856
e-mail: global@thinktwice.com
website: www.thinktwice.com

The ThinkTwice Global Vaccine Institute was established in 1996 to provide parents and other concerned people with educational resources enabling them to make more informed vaccine decisions. ThinkTwice encourages an uncensored exchange of vaccine information and supports every family's right to accept or reject vaccines. The institute has studies, articles, and books available at its website, including the book *Vaccine Safety Manual for Concerned Families and Health Practitioners.*

Vaccine Education Center
The Children's Hospital of Philadelphia
Thirty-fourth St. and Civic Center Blvd.
Philadelphia, PA 19104

(215) 590-9990
e-mail: vacinfo@email.chop.edu
website: www.vaccine.chop.edu

The Vaccine Education Center at the Children's Hospital of Philadelphia educates parents and health care providers about vaccines and immunizations. The center provides videos and information on every vaccine. Among the numerous publications available for download at the Vaccine Education Center's website is "Too Many Vaccines? What You Should Know."

Vaccine Liberation
PO Box 457
Spirit Lake, ID 83869-0457
(888) 249-1421
e-mail: vaclib@coldreams.com
website: www.vaclib.org

Vaccination Liberation is part of a national grassroots network dedicated to providing vaccination information not often made available to the public so that people can avoid and refuse vaccines. Vaccination Liberation works to dispute claims that vaccines are necessary, safe, and effective; expand awareness of alternatives in health care; preserve the right to abstain from vaccination; and repeal all compulsory vaccination laws nationwide. The organization has various information available at its website, including the article "How to Legally Avoid School Immunizations."

For Further Reading

Books

Allen, Arthur. *Vaccine: The Controversial Story of Medicine's Greatest Lifesaver.* New York: Norton, 2008. Discusses the history of the scientific development of vaccines and the accompanying social controversy surrounding vaccination.

Colgrove, James. *State of Immunity: The Politics of Vaccination in Twentieth-Century America.* Berkeley: University of California Press, 2006. Considers the unique ethical, political, and legal questions posed by having mandatory vaccinations for children.

Kirby, David. *Evidence of Harm: Mercury in Vaccines and the Autism Epidemic: A Medical Controversy.* New York: St. Martin's Griffin, 2006. Explores the heated controversy over what many parents, physicians, public officials, and educators have called an epidemic of autism in children, which many believe is linked to vaccines.

Link, Kurt. *The Vaccine Controversy: The History, Use, and Safety of Vaccinations.* Westport, CT: Praeger, 2005. A proponent of vaccination explores what he calls the paradox of the opposition to vaccination and discusses the powers, limitations, and risks of immunization.

Marshall, Gary. *The Vaccine Handbook.* Ann Arbor, MI: Professional Communications, 2008. Contains facts about diseases targeted by vaccines, rationale for vaccine use, vaccine efficacy and safety, and official recommendation for vaccine administration.

Miller, Neil Z. *Vaccine Safety Manual for Concerned Families and Health Practitioners.* Santa Fe, NM: New Atlantean, 2010. Discusses immunization risks and protections, including detailed information about every major vaccine.

————. *Vaccines: Are They Really Safe and Effective?* Santa Fe, NM: New Atlantean, 2008. Evaluates each vaccine for safety, efficacy, and long-term effects, and summarizes vaccine laws.

Myers, Martin, and Diego Pineda. *Do Vaccines Cause That?! A Guide for Evaluating Vaccine Safety Concerns.* Galveston, TX:

Immunizations for Public Health, 2008. Gives science-based answers to many questions about the safety of vaccines, discussing the risks and benefits of immunizations.

Offit, Paul. *Autism's False Prophets: Bad Science, Risky Medicine, and the Search for a Cure.* New York: Columbia University Press, 2008. Challenges the view that vaccines cause autism, exploring why society is susceptible to bad science.

————. *Vaccinated: One Man's Quest to Defeat the World's Deadliest Diseases.* New York: HarperCollins, 2008. Details microbiologist Maurice Hilleman's research and experiences as the basis for a larger exploration of the development of vaccines, covering two hundred years of medical history.

Tenpenny, Sherri J. *Saying No to Vaccines.* Middleburg Heights, OH: NMA Media-Press, 2008. Discusses the common misperceptions about vaccines and addresses problems with vaccines in all age groups, including vaccination requirements for adults.

Wakefield, Andrew J. *Callous Disregard: Autism and Vaccine—the Truth Behind a Tragedy.* New York: Skyhorse, 2010. Argues that the link between vaccination and autism has been denied because of corruption and profit motives.

Williamson, Stanley. *The Vaccination Controversy: The Rise, Reign, and Fall of Compulsory Vaccination for Smallpox.* Liverpool, UK: Liverpool University Press, 2008. Traces the origins of the vaccination controversy, raising issues related to the balance between personal liberties and societal obligations that remain relevant to contemporary debates about infant vaccination.

Periodicals and Internet Sources

Adams, Jill U. "Contagious Disease's Spread Highlights Dilemma over Unvaccinated Kids," *Los Angeles Times*, February 23, 2009.

Allen, Arthur. "Immune to Reason: Are Vaccine Skeptics Putting Your Kids at Risk?," *Mother Jones*, September/October 2008.

American Medical News. "Science Trumps Speculation: MMR Not Linked to Autism," April 6, 2009.

Bell, Alicia M. "Hold the Hype on HPV," *Women's Health Activist*, May/June 2007.

Bliss, Michael. "Fear's Old Struggle with Vaccination," *Globe & Mail* (Toronto, Canada), October 31, 2009.

Boodman, Sandra G. "Faith Lets Some Kids Skip Shots," *Washington Post*, June 10, 2008.

Childs, Frances. "How the Middle-Class MMR Refuseniks Are Putting Every Child at Risk," *Mail Online*, February 19, 2009. www.dailymail.co.uk.

Christian Science Monitor. "Keeping Choice on the Gardasil Vaccine," February 13, 2007.

Cohen, Marcus A. "Prevention of Cancer Associated with Human Papilloma Virus: A New Merck Vaccine vs. Nutritional Approaches," *Townsend Letter: The Examiner of Alternative Medicine*, June 2007.

Coombes, Rebecca. "Life Saving Treatment or Giant Experiment?," *British Medical Journal*, April 7, 2007.

Daley, Ellen M., and Robert J. McDermott. "The HPV Vaccine: Separating Politics from Science—a Commentary," *American Journal of Health Education*, May/June 2007.

Finch, Mark. "Point: Mandatory Influenza Vaccination for All Health Care Workers? Seven Reasons to Say 'No,'" *Clinical Infectious Diseases*, April 15, 2006.

Fumento, Michael. "A Merck-y Business: The Case Against Mandatory HPV Vaccinations," *Weekly Standard*, March 12, 2007.

Gapper, John. "The Hidden Cost of Free Vaccines," *Financial Times*, June 18, 2009.

Gerber, Renee. "Mandatory Cervical Cancer Vaccinations," *Journal of Law, Medicine, & Ethics*, Fall 2007.

Gostin, Lawrence O., and Catherine D. DeAngelis. "Mandatory HPV Vaccination: Public Health vs. Private Wealth," *JAMA*, May 2, 2007.

Grady, Denise. "A Vital Discussion, Clouded," *New York Times*, March 6, 2007.

Harrington, Penny. "Talking Points: The HPV Vaccine," Concerned Women for America, February 12, 2007. www.cwa.org.

Healy, Bernadine. "Don't Rush to Judgment," *U.S. News & World Report*, February 26, 2007.

Javitt, Gail H., Deena Berkowitz, and Lawrence O. Gostin. "Assessing Mandatory HPV Vaccination: Who Should Call the Shots?," *Journal of Law, Medicine, & Ethics*, Summer 2008.

Jeffrey, Terence. "Socializing Sexual Risk," *Townhall.com*, January 17, 2007. www.townhall.com.

Kalb, Claudia. "Stomping Through a Medical Minefield," *Newsweek*, October 25, 2008.

Klein, Sabra L., and Phyllis Greenberger. "Do Women Need Such Big Flu Shots?," *New York Times*, October 28, 2009.

Kluck, Shana. "Mandatory Vaccines Override Parental Rights," United Liberty, October 18, 2008. www.unitedliberty.org.

Lancet. "Should HPV Vaccines Be Mandatory for All Adolescents?," October 7, 2006.

McArdle, Megan. "The Poking Cure," *Atlantic Online*, March 28, 2008. www.theatlantic.com.

Miller, Neil Z. "7 Reasons Schools Should NOT Mandate Vaccines," ThinkTwice, 2008. www.thinktwice.com.

New York Times. "A Vaccine to Save Women's Lives," February 6, 2007.

Norsigian, Judy, Alicia Priest, and Robin Barnett. "Gardasil: What You Need to Know About the HPV Vaccine," *Network*, Spring/Summer 2007.

O'Beirne, Kate. "A Mandate in Texas: The Story of a Compulsory Vaccination and What It Means," *National Review Online*, March 5, 2007. www.nationalreview.com.

Offit, Paul A., and Charlotte A. Moser. "Nothing to Fear but the Flu Itself," *New York Times*, October 12, 2009.

———. "The Problem with Dr. Bob's Alternative Vaccine Schedule," *Pediatrics*, January 2009.

O'Rourke, Meghan. "Cancer Sluts: Does the HPV Vaccine 'Promote' Promiscuity?," *Slate*, September 27, 2007. www.slate.com.

Perry, Rick. "My Order Protects Life," *USA Today*, February 8, 2007.

Phillips, Alan G. "Refusal to Vaccinate Forms Raise Ethical Questions," *Townsend Letter: The Examiner of Alternative Medicine*, May 2008.

Picard, Andre. "Why Politics and Public Health Don't Mix," *Globe & Mail* (Toronto, Canada), February 21, 2008.

Pratt, Andrew Plemmons. "Safe Vaccines and Healthy Children: An Interview with Dr. Saad B. Omer on Vaccine Policy," *Science Progress*, May 2, 2008. www.scienceprogress.org.

Reynolds, Glenn Harlan. "As Diseases Make Comeback, Why Aren't All Kids Vaccinated?," *Popular Mechanics*, August 1, 2008.

Schlafly, Phyllis. "Universal Child Care Poses Threat to Parental Rights," *Human Events*, January 14, 2008. www.humanevents.com.

Sprigg, Peter. "Pro-Family, Pro-vaccine—But Keep It Voluntary," *Washington Post*, July 15, 2006.

Staver, Mathew D. "Compulsory Vaccinations Threaten Religious Freedom," Liberty Counsel, 2007.

USA Today. "Rush to Require Cancer Shot Threatens to Promote Backlash," February 8, 2007.

Walker, Jesse. "Injecting Speed: Why the Rush to Require the HPV Vaccine," *Reason Online*, February 20, 2007. www.reason.com.

Washington Times. "Inoculating," February 28, 2007.

————. "The Upside to Flu Shots: For Most, It's Better to Be Safe Than Sorry," October 15, 2009.

Wente, Margaret. "Autism, Vaccines, and Fear," *Globe & Mail* (Toronto, Canada), February 4, 2010.

Whelan, Elizabeth M. "Cancer Triumph and Travail," *Washington Times*, June 15, 2006.

Websites

Vaccination Risk Awareness Network (www.vran.org). This website provides information about the risks and potential side effects of vaccines.

World Association for Vaccine Education (www.novaccine.com). This website provides information about mass vaccination systems.

World Health Organization (www.who.org). The website of the World Health Organization contains information about vaccination programs worldwide.

Index

A

AAP (American Academy of
    Pediatrics), 8
Adverse drug reactions, 16
    underreporting of, 17
AIDS treatment, percent
    receiving in developing
    world, 108
AIDS vaccine
    more time/money should be
        invested in, 100–104
    no more research money
        should be spent on,
        105–110
    potential impact of, 104*t*
    views of leading researchers
        on, *109*
American Academy of Pediatrics
    (AAP), 8
American Psychiatric
    Association, 7
And the Band Played On (Shilts),
    28
ASDs. *See* Autism spectrum
    disorders
Atlanta Journal-Constitution
    (newspaper), 49
Atlantic (magazine), 37, 38
Autism Speaks, 31, 32–33, 34
Autism/autism spectrum
    disorders (ASDs), 7
    are not linked to vaccines,
        31–35

may be linked to vaccines,
    24–30
trend in number of cases, *29*
Autism's False Prophets (Offit),
    57
AVERT, 108

B

Babies (birth to 18 months),
    number of vaccination
    received, 14, *15, 16*
Baker, Bevan, 44, 46
Baltimore, David, 106
Barry, John M., 88
Beck, Glen, 42
Berkley, Seth, 100, 106
Blaxill, Mark, 29
Blaylock, Russell, 15–16
Buffalo News (newspaper), 61

C

Callous Disregard (Wakefield), 8
Canada, impact of H1N1
    pandemic in, 78
Cave, Stephanie, 16
Centers for Disease Control and
    Prevention (CDC), 44, 89,
    96
    on autism spectrum disorders,
        7, 13, 32
    on compliance rates for
        childhood vaccinations, 49
    on deaths from H1N1, 73

on extent of H1N1
pandemic, 42, 86
on increase in measles cases,
57
infant vaccine
recommendations by, 14
Cervical cancer vaccine, 19–20,
21
Childhood vaccinations
compliance rates for, 49
numbers received from birth
to 18 months, *16*
parental perspectives on, *34*
survey on parental refusal of,
58
Coalition for SafeMinds, 8
Columbia Journalism Review
(journal), 27
Condon, Bradley, 90

D
Dalrymple, Theodore, 18
Department of Health and
Human Services, US (HHS),
86
*Diagnostic and Statistical
Manual of Mental Disorders*
(*DSM-IV-TR*, American
Psychiatric Association), 7
Donald, Leslie, 72

E
Eisenstein, Mayer, 27
Ethyl mercury (thimerosal), 8,
12, 27, 28, 33

F
FDA (Food and Drug
Administration, US), 8, 13

Flu vaccines
against all strains are needed,
88–93
are safe/vital to public health,
41–46
effectiveness of, 91
evidence of effectiveness is
not conclusive, 36–40
health care workers, all should
get, 61–65
new technology is needed to
end shortages of, 82–87
percentage of health care
workers receiving, *70*
should not be mandatory for
health care workers, 66–71
See also H1N1 vaccine
Food and Drug Administration,
US (FDA), 8, 13
Ford, Gerald, 45, 98
Fullerton, Michael, 36

G
Generation Rescue, 26
GlaxoSmithKline (GSK), 95
Globe and Mail (newspaper), 77
GSK (GlaxoSmithKline), 95
Guichon, Juliet, 76
Guillain-Barré syndrome, 42,
45–46, 96

H
H1N1 (swine flu) pandemic
deaths/illness from, 73, 83
declaration of, 37, 89
extent of, 86
perceptions of federal
response to, *98*

H1N1 vaccine
  decision against is selfish,
    76–80
  decision on is personal, 72–76
  health care workers should
    get, 61–65
  problems with supply of, 92
  public opinion on, *74*
  and seasonal flu vaccine
    parents' plans on children
      getting, *43*
    percentage of health care
      workers receiving, *64*
  views on shortage of, *85*
Haggard, Henry Rider, 21
Hardin, Garrett, 77
Health Canada, 74
HHS (Department of Health
  and Human Services, US),
  86
HIV (human immunodeficiency
  virus)
  daily number of new
    infections, 103
  prevention of transmission is
    best approach to, 107–108
  testing for, 55
  worldwide numbers living
    with/newly infected with,
    103
  See also AIDS vaccine
Human immunodeficiency
  virus. *See* AIDS treatment;
  AIDS vaccine; HIV

I
Immunization Safety Review
  Committee (Institute of
  Medicine), 8–9

Independent (newspaper), 110
Influenza
  means of transmission, 69
  See also Flu vaccines; H1N1
    vaccine; Pandemics
Institute of Medicine (IOM),
  8–9
International AIDS Vaccine
  Initiative, 103
*International Journal of
  Epidemiology*, 38

J
Jackson, Lisa, 38
Jaeger, Gustav, 21
Jefferson, Tom, 39–40

K
Kalb, Claudia, 31
Kessler, David, 17
Khanlou, Homayoon, 105
King, Mike, 48

L
Lancet (journal), 7–8
Law & Order (TV program), 57
Legionnaire's disease, 97
Lewis, David, 96, 98
Lieberman, Jeffrey A., 25
Link, Kurt, 7

M
Maggiore, Christine, 57
Maher, Bill, 42
Majumdar, Sumit, 38
Maloney, Carolyn, 26, *26*
Measles, *50*
  death rate from, 57
  increase in cases of, 49

mumps, and rubella vaccine (MMR), 7–8, 14, 28, 33

Media
portrayal of non-vaccinators in, 57–58
vaccine-autism link in, 27–28

Mercury. *See* Ethyl mercury

Miller, Henry I., 83

Miller, Neil Z., 11

Milwaukee Journal Sentinel (newspaper), 41

Mitchell, Ian, 76

MMR (measles, mumps, and rubella) vaccine, 7–8, 14, 28, 33

Morton, Natalie, 19, 21

N

National Institutes of Health (NIH), 90

New England Journal of Medicine, 42

New York State Nurses Association, 66

NIH (National Institutes of Health), 90

O

Obama, Barack, *45*

Offit, Paul A., 57

Olmsted, Dan, 24

O'Mara, Peggy, 54

Opinion polls. *See* Surveys

Ostrom, Elinor, 80

P

Pandemics, influenza
common features of, 89

mass vaccination efforts are problematic in dealing with, 94–99
See also H1N1 pandemic; Spanish flu pandemic

Parents, fears about vaccines among, 51–52

Parry, Vivienne, 94

Patterson, David A., 62

Pediatrics (journal), 59

Polio, 7
trend in number of cases, *22*

Polls. *See* Surveys

Preston, Kelly, 57

Private Practice (TV program), 57

ProQuad vaccine, 28–29

R

Recombinant DNA technology (gene-splicing), 84–86

S

Santa Fe New Mexican (newspaper), 59

Science (journal), 77

Sebelius, Kathleen, 44

Shaw, George Bernard, 21

Shilts, Randy, 28

Singer, Alison, 31

Sinha, Tapen, 90

Smallpox, 7, 21

Spanish flu pandemic (1918–1920), 90

Statistics Canada, 78

Surveys
of AIDS researchers on AIDS vaccine, 108, *109,* 110

Picture Credits

AP Images, 97

AP Images/Ed Andrieski, 33

AP Images/David Cheskin/PA Wire, 56

AP Images/Darron Cummings, 63, 68

AP Images/Ana P. Gutierrez, 73

AP Images/Harry Hamburg, 26

AP Images/Idaho Press-Tribune/Mike Vogt, 39

AP Images/Sakchai Lalit, 107

AP Images/Miguel Tovar, 91

AP Images/Rui Vieira, 20

AP Images/The White House/Pete Souza, 45

BSIP/Photo Researchers, Inc., 15

Gale/Cengage Learning, 16, 22, 29, 34, 43, 58, 64, 70, 74, 85, 98, 104, 109

Dr. P. Marazzi/Photo Researchers, Inc., 50

Maximilian Stock Ltd./Photo Researchers, Inc., 81

David Parker/Photo Researchers, Inc., 102

Phanie/Photo Researchers, Inc., 10

Tek Image/Photo Researchers, Inc., 84

Fred Thornhill/Reuters/Landov, 79

Gu Xinrong/Xinhua/Landov, 47